THE LIFE
of the Mind

THE LIFE
of the Mind

On the Joys and Travails
of Thinking

James V. Schall

ISI BOOKS
WILMINGTON, DELAWARE

Schall, James V.

    The life of the mind : on the joys and travails of thinking / James V. Schall. — 1st paperback ed. —Wilmington, Del. : ISI Books, c2008.

        p. ; cm.

        ISBN: 978-1-933859-61-3 (pbk.)
        First published in 2006.
        Includes bibliographical references and index.

        1. Thought and thinking. 2. Thought and thinking—Philosophy. 3. Intellect—Philosophy. 4. Philosophy. I. Title.

BF441 .S269 2008   2007942039
128.3—dc22   0802

Book Design by Kelly Cole
Manufactured in the United States of America

Published in the United States by:

    ISI Books
    Intercollegiate Studies Institute
    Post Office Box 4431
    Wilmington, DE 19807-0431
    www.isibooks.org

One's existence as a spiritual being
involves being and remaining oneself and at
the same time admitting and transforming into oneself
the reality of the world. . . . But where there is mind, the totality
of things has room; it is "possible that in a single being the
comprehensiveness of the whole universe may dwell"
(Aquinas, *De Veritate*, 2, 2).

—Josef Pieper, *Contemplation and Happiness*

For if I grew up no better instructed about
the world of books than was Columbus about global geography,
I had in store for me, as he did, the splendors of discovery.

—Phyllis McGinley, "The Consolations of Illiteracy"

Contents

Acknowledgments

For permission to reprint here certain chapters in revised form, I offer thanks to the Catholic University of America Press (chapter I); *Vital Speeches* (chapter II); Rockhurst University Press (chapter III); *Fellowship of Catholic Scholars Quarterly* (chapter VIII); *Logos* (chapter IX); *Motions, University of San Diego Law Journal* (chapter X); *National Review Online* (appendix II); and *Homiletic and Pastoral Review* (appendix III).

Introduction

A Certain Lightness in Existence

The title, subtitle, and two introductory citations of this book contain four thematic elements—the "life of the mind," the "joys and travails of thinking," the "splendor of discovery," and the potential existence in ourselves of all things not ourselves. The notion of precisely the "splendor" of discovery is something that I found in the poet Phyllis McGinley, though it is an ancient idea. It does not merely mean that things exist, or even, as Étienne Gilson once said, that "things exist and I know them." It includes the additional element that we see a light, as it were, shining through all reality, something that incites us to respond to it, to behold it. There is a radiance to being. All things that are limited to themselves point to what is not themselves.

Although I was at first inclined to title this book *The Splendor of Discovery,* I finally decided to call it *The Life of the Mind,* a title I quite liked. But a friend in Australia reminded me that this title, *The Life of the Mind,* had also been given to a famous two-volume study by the great German philosopher, Hannah Arendt. I had to laugh at this reminder, as I have on my shelves both volumes of this work, devoted respectively to "Thinking" and "Willing." The final volume, "Judging," never appeared. Indeed I had reviewed this book.[1] Arendt's volume titles are familiar to anyone who knows Plato, Aristotle, Augustine, or Aquinas. Arendt was indeed most influenced by Augustine, about whom she wrote her doctorate. What could be more insightful than the following sentence? "The true opposite of factual, as distinguished from rational, truth is not error or illusion but the deliberate lie."[2]

My "life of the mind" is not that of Arendt, of course, but she is right. The lie is opposed to the true statement of *what is*, just as error is opposed to valid reasoning. The life of the mind is indeed concerned with distinguishing lies from truth, error from reason. We want to know these things—what is truth? what is error? what is reasonable? what is a lie?—for their own sakes, because that activity of knowing these things is our life; it is our mind. In the end, *The Life of the Mind*, as I hope will become clear, still seems to be the best description of what I have to say here.

This book, be it affirmed in the beginning, lest there be doubt, is not a study about a physical organ called the brain, nor is it a book in logic—of how concepts are related to each other. Any bibliographical or research check online or in a library will reveal, besides the Arendt books, numerous other books and papers with this same title, "the life of the mind," dealing with sundry aspects of knowing or with the physical organ, the brain.

That our minds are alive, that they have a "life," is a classic philosophic principle. *Vivere viventibus est esse*, that is, the very being of living things is that such things do live. They have a source of motion within themselves, their own peculiar activity. Likewise, some living things, ourselves included, also have minds. The very "life" of beings with intelligence is *to think*, to exercise this intelligence actively, on *what is*. A knowing being lives most acutely, most vividly, when it thinks about *what is*.

Our minds initially are empty. While empty, even before we think anything, they are minds, that is, knowing powers we did not give ourselves. Until they encounter something not themselves, something outside of themselves, our minds do not know anything. The mind is a power that actively seeks to know what is there, what it encounters.

More precisely, what knows is not the mind but we ourselves with or through our minds. Nothing, furthermore, is really complete unless it is also known. All things have two existences, a real one and a mental one. The mental one is really a quality of the existing being who is thinking about what, outside of himself, is known through his mind.

We can, however, know something but not really be moved by it. We can choose not to think deeply about it. Chesterton once said, in a memorable phrase of which I am inordinately fond, that there is no such thing as an uninteresting subject, only uninterested people. Nothing is so unimportant that it is not worth knowing. Everything reveals something. Our minds cannot fully exhaust the reality contained in even the smallest existing thing.

The condition of our being human, then, is the risk of not knowing something worth knowing. The "whole universe may dwell in our minds," as Aquinas remarked. This indwelling is the purpose for which we are given minds in the first place. What makes it all right to be a particular, finite human being, such as each of us is, is that, because of intelligence, the universe is also given back to each of us. Our knowing does not take anything away from what is known. Nor does our individual knowing take anything away from others knowing the same thing in the same universe.

What is given to us besides ourselves seems initially given that we might simply behold it. This is what Aristotle meant when he defined the mind as that power that is capable of knowing all things. This primary contemplative moment does not imply that we can have no further purpose or use for what we know. Knowledge enables us to act in the world for our immediate and ultimate purposes. Nonetheless, what is there to be known usually antedates our own finite existence. We know ourselves first as receivers of what is there to be known without us.

This is a book about thinking and reading, about thinking while reading, about being aware and being delighted in the very acts of either reading or thinking. It is, if you will, a book in the famous *artes liberales*, in the liberal arts. That is, it deals with those things that free us to be what we are, what we are intended to be, beings who know, who know *what is*, who delight in this knowing. We are not to be afraid of the splendors in things, except perhaps in the fear that, granted our finiteness and, more darkly, our reluctant wills, we may miss some of them.

Some advice will be found here about what to read and why to read. At the end, there is a particular book list designed to "waken" our minds. If there is a sense of urgency, of not wanting to miss anything, even if, till now, we have missed many things, it is not set over against the leisure in which we have time for things. We want to know things that are beyond ourselves, that are not ourselves, almost as if this knowing others is part of knowing ourselves, as I think it is. We are not given ourselves as if we were only to be concerned with ourselves. Yet, we are receivers; we are given things so that we might know them. We are even told to "know ourselves," no mean feat as the history of philosophy and our own experience teaches us.

Indeed, as I shall often suggest, we cannot and do not know ourselves unless we first know what is not ourselves. We become "alive" in the intellectual sense by knowing even the humblest thing, no less than the greatest, both of which can fascinate us. But with both the great and the small we can also choose to ignore, even reject them. We suspect that there is a connection between the highest of things and the lowest and what is in between—in which latter category, if we are wise, we place ourselves. The Greeks, indeed, called us "the mortals," the beings who die and, uniquely, know that they die. They also called us the *microcosmoi,* the tiny (micro) individual beings in whom somehow the whole of creation exists, in all its levels, matter, life, sense, mind.

Indeed, I will even suggest that, paradoxically, there is a danger in not being delighted with our knowing of *what is*. We are to be pleased about those things that are, in their own order, pleasing. It is a perversion of both mind and heart to think that somehow *what is,* is not also given to us. I am bold enough to maintain, with Belloc, that even while walking, we can and do encounter the things *that are*. There is a "metaphysics" in the privilege of walking this green earth. It may be advantageous, moreover, to have had a "bad education," as Phyllis McGinley tells us, if it leads us to seek out what we missed. Plato is quite careful not to rush us along too soon in our learning. He implies that our relatively little time as mortals is enough time to accomplish—make manifest—what we are. We do not, as we recall from the end of the *Republic*, have an opportunity to choose our "daimon," our destiny, a second time. We are given one life. It is enough.

This is, as it were, a book for those who, while being educated, often with the highest credentials, were not exposed to the highest things and who, in spite of it all, suspect that they are lacking something. This book follows on my previous books on what can be broadly called "education and reality"—*Another Sort of Learning, A Student's Guide to Liberal Learning*, and *On the Unseriousness of Human Affairs*.

One chapter hints that we need "to take care of our own wisdom." Another talks about the "whole risk of being a human being": the risk, as it were, is that we are given so much but do not realize it. Yes, we can choose to miss what is there. This is not an "academic" book, though, hopefully, it is an intelligent one. If there is a certain lightsomeness in these considerations, it is because there is *a certain lightsomeness in existence itself*, something we miss at our peril. Things do "depend" on a philosophy that knows *of what is, that it is.*

This is not a "self-help" book, to recall Walker Percy's acerbic and delightful *Lost in the Cosmos: The Last Self-Help Book.*[3] Even less is it a book on "self-reliance" or "self-transcendence" or "self-interest." It is rather a book of wonder, of amazement that something really exists, including one's self. I am much taken by the "order of things," both that there is order and that I can know it, discover it. I do not "make the world," but find it already there, already what it is. Hence, I speak of "discovery," not "making." It is a great comfort, on honestly knowing ourselves, to acknowledge that we do not cause *what is* to be. And if I speak of the "life of the mind," I do not mean that this life is unrelated to or totally independent of the life of the senses within the body. We exist as a whole. We are single beings both in what we are and in what we know.

Thus, I begin with a reflection on A. D. Sertillanges' famous book *The Intellectual Life*, because such a life is something we all can and want to strive for, even the humblest of us. Thomas Aquinas, who possessed perhaps the best mind of our kind, did not hesitate to spend time with the slower of his brothers in teaching them what they could know. But he himself spent most of his waking hours in the careful, profound, and incisive explication of *what is*. He did not neglect any source of information that is available to us, including revelation.

Does this book have a "practical" purpose? Will it help you get into graduate school, or get a better job, or run for office? Not really. It is largely addressed to what is impractical about us, to what has to do with knowing, not doing, even granting their intimate relationship. The "doing" that I envision is not merely the desire to find a book and to read it. It is to feel our soul moved by what is not ourselves, by the truth, by *what is*. Plato, in a famous passage in his Seventh Letter, warned us about writing, about how its set words could conceal what it is that they are meant to reveal or convey. He claimed that he never wrote what he really thought. He told us that he only wrote Socratic dialogues, though he did unexpectedly confess in the *Symposium* that he did know something about love. In reading Plato's dialogues, we ought to be led to the vision that he had, if we be philosophers.

St. Thomas also understood that we can never fully understand or state the whole truth of anything or of everything. Yet, he thought that we could and should say what it is we know, realizing, with Socrates, that the reality will be more than our words and concepts can convey. Both Plato and Thomas set us on an adventure, a search, a quest simply to know. If we have allowed ourselves to be dulled, to be deflected from reality, these pages, it is hoped, will serve to awaken us, to resume in our souls that vocation we all have to know, as best we can, *what is*.

Chapter I

ON THE JOYS AND TRAVAILS OF THINKING

A vocation is not fulfilled by vague reading and a few
scattered writings.
                                        —A. D. Sertillanges

Many of us in later years wish that someone would have told us, when
we were younger, about certain things, often certain books, which, as we
look back on it, would have greatly helped us in the project of our lives.
In particular, certain books, we suspect, would have at least helped us
know the truth of things. Some of these books are directed to what is
true, to reality, to *what is*. But a certain number of others, such as Aristotle's
Organon, are directed to the question of the elements of knowing and
speaking, or how we ought to go about knowing. I have in fact written
one such book myself, *Another Sort of Learning*. In that book, I mention
A. D. Sertillanges' book on "the intellectual life" to be among those few
books that will give anyone seriously interested a good start.

But Sertillanges gives more than a good start. He explicitly tells us
how to begin, how to read and write, how to discipline our time, even
our souls. He also attends to the life of the spirit in which any true intellectual life exists. We have perhaps heard from Aristotle that we are rational animals, that the contemplative life is something to which we should

aspire. Practically no one tells us what this life might mean, whether it is something that is available to us on some condition that we do not easily comprehend. But even if we vaguely know that the intellectual life is an exalted one, we have heard rather less about what acquiring this life might entail. No one spells out its terms and conditions. We are also aware that wisdom comes somewhat later in life than we might at first have suspected or desired. Yet, we surmise that ways existed that could have helped us had we only known them.

Sertillanges' *La Vie Intellectuelle*, first published in 1921, was an immediate success. It went through many editions, in many languages, and thanks to the Catholic University of America Press, is still in print.

I want to explain why this book should always be sought out by young undergraduate and graduate students, by elderly folks, and by everyone in between. Every time I have used this book in a class, often when I teach a St. Thomas Aquinas course, I have had undergraduate students tell me later that it was a book they remembered. It taught them much about how to maintain their intellectual curiosity in a practical, effective manner not merely in college but throughout their lives. Thus, at the beginning of this book, the best way I can go about my effort to talk of "the life of the mind" is to advise the reading of another book, not necessarily immediately, but still soon enough, a book with almost the same title, *The Intellectual Life*. In the "life of the mind" it is all right, even exciting, if one book leads us to another—if one author leads us to a second one.

At first sight, *The Intellectual Life* is a "quaint" book. At second sight, it is an utterly demanding book.[1] Sertillanges painstakingly tells us how to take notes, how to begin to write and publish, how to organize our notes and, behind them, our thoughts, even our days. It seems "quaint" because we no longer use, as Sertillanges did, pens or typewriters. We are grateful for the opportunity to use late-model computers and printing processes that would have amazed him. But Sertillanges' advice is just as pertinent and demanding for someone with a computer as it is for someone with a pencil.

We need to recall that many of the greatest books and writings were initially put down on parchment or even stone. If we look at the total output of great thinkers like Aristotle or Augustine or Aquinas, it is difficult to imagine how they could have been more productive even if they had had a computer. Human mind and ingenuity, evidently, will find a way to record what is worth setting down. After all, what is important is what is true, not the mechanics of recording it. In the 1920s, Sertillanges himself was far better off technologically than was Aquinas, about whom Sertillanges wrote so well. Technological capacity, however useful, is not the same as intelligence. The truth alone is reason enough to look at Sertillanges' book, and through it, at Aquinas, from whom also this present book derives so much.

"How did Aquinas ever do it?" we wonder. It is highly doubtful, as I have said, that he would have written more or better if he had had the latest computer and research tools at his disposal. In fact, in some sense, such things may have been a hindrance. For St. Thomas Aquinas developed a great memory and an uncanny capacity to have at his fingertips the teachings of the great writers before his time, including Scripture. This wisdom took books and reading, of course, even for Aquinas, but he learned how to do these things. What Sertillanges teaches us is how, in our own way, to imitate the lessons imparted by the life of the great Dominican—how to lead a proper intellectual life, one suffused with honesty, prayer, diligent work, and, in the end, the delight of knowing.

In reading Sertillanges' book, a first outside project that I now recommend, we cannot help feeling that he is letting us in on some of the secrets of Aquinas's vast productivity and keen insight. There are just so many hours in the day, week, or month. Sertillanges does not ask us all to give up our daily lives and devote ourselves full-time to the intellectual life in the sense that St. Thomas Aquinas did. Rather, in his practical way, Sertillanges teaches us how to organize our lives so that we can acquire a solid beginning, hopefully when we are young, and spend the rest of our days building on this solid foundation. In brief, Sertillanges teaches us about habits, about discipline, productivity, and truth. He thinks that we can lead a truly intellectual life if we manage to keep one or two hours a day for serious pursuit of the higher things. He is not rigid or impractical here. Moreover, when stated merely in terms of hours or time, we tend to miss what Sertillanges is driving at.

Any sort of learning, in the beginning, will have drudgery connected with it. We can simply call it a kind of work. We need to come to a point where we begin to delight in what we are knowing, where we cannot wait to get back to our considerations or writings or thoughts on a given topic. Anything *that is* is fascinating. Chesterton, whose own intellectual life seems as vibrant as anyone in modern times, remarked that there are no such things as uninteresting subjects, only uninterested people. This is one of those truths which is so obvious that we can hardly bear it, since it forces us to look first to ourselves for the cause of our boredom. A large part of this "uninterestedness" happens precisely because we have never learned how or why to see what is there. Sertillanges teaches us to examine our lives. He does not neglect to mention that moral faults, both serious and light ones, can in fact hinder or prevent us from having the freedom from ourselves that enables us to see what is not ourselves, to see *what is*. "Do you want to have an intellectual life?" Sertillanges asks in his introduction to the 1934 edition. "Begin by creating within you a zone of silence." We live in a world surrounded by noise, by a kind of strident unrest that fills our days and nights. We have so many things to distract us, even if sometimes we think they might educate us. Sertillanges is sure we have the time. But he is also sure that we do not notice that we have time because our lives appear to be busy and full. We find the time first by becoming interested, by longing to know. Sertillanges demands an examination of conscience both about our sins and about our use of time.

An intellectual life, a contemplative life, is itself filled with activity, but activity that is purposeful, that wants to know and to know the truth. Those we often call "intellectuals" today are probably not exactly what Sertillanges had in mind when he talked about "the intellectual life." Intellectuals as a class, as Paul Johnson wrote in his book *The*

Intellectuals, may well devise their theories and explanations precisely as products of, or justifications for, their own moral disorders. They are the modern-day versions of the sophists Plato criticized so much for not taking a stand on the truth of things. We should never forget that an intellectual life can be a dangerous life. The greatest of vices stem not from the flesh but from the spirit, as Augustine said. The brightest of the angels was the fallen angel.

These sober considerations explain why I like this little book by Sertillanges, why I take the trouble to talk about it at the beginning of this book. He does not hesitate to warn us of the intimate relation between our knowing the truth and the ordering of our own souls to the good. The intellectual life can be and often is a perilous life. But this is no reason to deny its glory. And Sertillanges is very careful to direct us to those things that we pursue because they explain what we are, explain the world and God to us. A first step in having a life of the mind is to know that other minds have had lives, which they explain to us—if we would listen.

When we pick up Sertillanges' book, we will be surprised, no doubt, by its detailed practicality. It is not totally unlike Fowler's *Modern English Usage* or Strunk and White's *Elements of Style*. In another sense, this is a handbook, a step-by-step direction of what to do first, what next. We are tempted to think that the intellectual life is some gigantic insight that comes to us one fine morning while we are shaving or making breakfast. Sertillanges does not deny that some insight can come this way, but the normal course of things requires us habitually to pursue the truth, to know, to be curious about reality.

The Intellectual Life, moreover, is not primarily for academic professionals, though it will harm not a single one of them. Nor would I say it is for everyone. But it is for very many and not just for those who have advanced degrees in physics or metaphysics. This is a book that allows us to be free and independent, to know why we need not be dependent on the media or any ideology. It is a book that does not exactly "teach" us to know, but it does teach us how to go about knowing and how to continue knowing. It is designed to keep us inwardly alive precisely by teaching us how to know and grow in knowing, steadily, patiently, and yes, critically.

I would put *The Intellectual Life* on the desk of every serious student, and most of the unserious ones. Indeed, Plato said that our very lives are "unserious" in comparison to that of God. Something of that relaxed leisure, of that serene sense of freedom that comes from knowing and wanting to know is instilled in our souls by this book. Its very presence on our desk or shelves is a constant prod, a visible reminder to us that the intellectual life is not something alien, not something that we have no chance, in our own way, to learn about.

We should read through this classic book, making its teachings ours after our own manner. Adapting what Sertillanges suggests to our own computer habits, to our own books, to our own hours of the day or night should be no problem. The book will have an abiding, concrete effect on our lives. If we follow its precepts, it will make us alive in that inner, curious, delightful way connoted by the words in its magnificent title—*The Intellectual Life*. I see no reason for settling for anything less. The great French Dominican still teaches us how to learn, but only if we are free enough to let him teach us—only if we are free enough to want to know.

Chapter II

Books and the Intellectual Life

I

Thus far, we have seen that one way to begin attending to the "life of the mind" is with *The Intellectual Life*. We have also mentioned in passing, Fowler, Strunk and White, Phyllis McGinley, Thomas Aquinas, Chesterton, Aristotle, Josef Pieper, Walker Percy, Étienne Gilson, Plato, and Paul Johnson. Now we come to *Samuel* Johnson. Some years ago, in 1979, when I first began teaching at Georgetown, I happened to read in class something by Johnson, the great English lexicographer and philosopher. I no longer recall quite what I read, though I am habitually prepared to read something by Johnson at the drop of a hat. Most days, I try to read for myself something from his unfailing wisdom. At any rate, several months after that initial encounter I received in the mail, from Florida, a package that contained a 1931 reprint of a book originally printed in the year 1799.

The book was James Boswell's *Life of Samuel Johnson, L.L.D.* This two-volume-in-one book was found by a student in that 1979 class in some used bookstore—used bookstores, I am going to insist here, are places to be haunted by young students as almost the equivalent of

Stevenson's *Treasure Island*, for they are indeed usually full of unexpected treasures, if you know what to look for. The particular book I had been sent, as a blue-inked stamp on its title page informs us, once was housed in St. Paul's High School Library in St. Petersburg, Florida. Surely any high school or university library that gets rid of such a marvelous book deserves to lose, if not its accreditation, its reputation! I think of this incident each year when I notice what basic books—say, Aristotle's *Ethics* or Plato's *Republic*—students sell back to the university bookstore as used, certain signs of intellectual failure on the part of the students selling them back. I would add that worthless books *should* be sold back—the trick is to know the difference.

To build on what I have said about *The Intellectual Life* in the previous chapter, let me here provide some reflections on books—on acquiring them, on keeping them, on reading them, and on re-reading them. Never forget C. S. Lewis's perceptive remark that if you have only read a great book once, you have not read it at all (though you must read it once in order to be able to read it again). In his *An Experiment in Criticism*, Lewis wrote, "Those who read great works . . . will read the same work ten, twenty, or thirty times during the course of their life."[1] Furthermore, he adds, "We must never assume that we know exactly what is happening when anyone else reads a book."[2] The same book can move another's will and understanding differently than it does our own. We ourselves are receptive to different books at different times in our lives. It is quite possible for one to get nothing out of reading a book, whereas someone else, reading the same book, goes out and changes the world. Likewise we can be excited by reading a book that our friends find dull. There is a mystery here of how mind speaks to mind through reading.

But back to Samuel Johnson and one of his statements about books, a passage on which I often reflect. In his immensely insightful book, Boswell recalls several observations that Johnson made on Monday, September 22, 1777. "Dr. Johnson advised me to-day," Boswell begins, to have as many books about me as I could; that I might read upon any subject upon which I had a desire for instruction at the time. "What you read *then* said he, you will remember, but if you have not a book immediately ready, and the subject moulds in your mind, it is a chance if you again have a desire to study it." He added, "if a man never has an eager desire for instruction, he should prescribe a task for himself. But it is better when a man reads from immediate inclination." (II, 148)

I note what Johnson advises here. Do not let things "mould," that is, grow stale and inert in our minds so that we never think of them again. Johnson suggests that we keep ready about us plenty of books on many a subject matter; that is, we need our own basic library, one that we own because we have ourselves found and purchased the books in it.

But just having lots of books is not enough. Fools can own libraries. The devil was one of the most intelligent of the angels and we know what happened to him. Knowledge alone won't save us, though we need knowledge too. The essential thing is the "inclination to know," something that cannot be purchased or borrowed or injected. Johnson suggests that we can, to some extent, prod ourselves to know; as he puts it, we can ascribe a "task for ourselves." We can, for instance, say to ourselves, "I will read *The Brothers Karamazov* during Christmas vacation," and then do it. But it is best to have an "eager desire for instruction," something that flows from our own inner resources, not just from external duty. If we read the first paragraph of *The Brothers Karamazov* and have any soul at all, we will not rest till we finish it.

I can hardly emphasize enough that, ultimately, each must discover in his own soul this longing to know. Nothing can replace it. This longing to know constitutes the very heart of what we are as rational beings, distinct in the universe precisely because we ourselves can know. In the last analysis, we have to wake up to knowledge. We cannot do that, as Plato hinted, till we reach a certain level of maturity or self-discipline. An experienced teacher can almost tell, by the light in his eyes, the day a student first wakes up and begins to want to know. No one can really find a substitute for his own personal attraction to the truth itself. If this desire is not there, no one can give it to us from outside ourselves. And if it is not there, it is undoubtedly because we have not ordered ourselves or put our interests aside long enough to wonder about things, about things "for their own sakes," as Aristotle put it. I admit, however, that vanity can sometimes help. If we are finally embarrassed for the fiftieth time to have to admit that we never read Aristotle's *Poetics* or Chesterton's *Orthodoxy*, we may finally read them merely to appear cultured, only to be surprised to learn how good they are.

II

Let us recall that no limit can be assigned to what we can know. It is a mistake to think that when we learn something it is at the expense of something else. Knowledge is not a zero-sum game. It is, indeed, one of the greatest of the riches of the universe. Our soul is not a material, finite receptacle; it operates with a properly spiritual power. It is true that we need to apportion our time and efforts, that some things are more fascinating than others. But in principle, all things, no matter how insignificant, are worth knowing. If we find ourselves bored, it is not because there are no interesting things about us to know. Our minds have what the ancients called a "*capax omnium.*" They have a capacity to know all things. This is a phrase that I shall often repeat. Aristotle has a good discussion of it in the Third Book of his *De Anima*. It is through knowing that that which is not ourselves, that *which is* in itself, becomes ours. It becomes a proper addition to what we are; for us, to know is also to be.

Indeed, it is through knowing what is not ourselves that we can come to realize, reflexively, our own selves—our own very existence and activity. We become luminous to ourselves only when we know what is not ourselves. In a sense, the whole world is offered to us in order that we can know ourselves. We are the one thing in the variegated universe that we cannot directly know. We can look at our faces in mirrors, but we can only know our minds while they are knowing something else. The universe ultimately gives us to ourselves. But to know, we need time, discipline, and an order of knowing, as St. Thomas Aquinas told us in the beginning of the great *Summa Theologiae*. The adventure of knowing is our avenue to the adventure of being—to the being of all things *that are*.

To take a rather amusing example of how many odd things we can know, let me ask, at random, what is a vitologist? Or better, what is vitolphilia? If we know our Greek suffixes, we know that "philia" means the love of something. At its highest meaning, as Aristotle tells us, it means the love of our friend; better, it means the mutual love of one another. But in this context, vitolphilia means the love of what? Well, I would never have heard of this obscure word had it not been for the fact that someone gave me for Christmas one of those daily throwaway calendars dedicated to—of all things—cigars. (Of course, I never smoke cigars myself without turning green in the process.) This puzzling word was just sitting around on my desk waiting for the right day to arrive—in this case, Wednesday, January 13, 1999. It turns out that the first part of the word vitolphilia refers to the artwork on cigar boxes or on the bands around cigars called vitolas. In fact, in Havana there is a large museum that displays the intricate artwork, from the eighteenth century on, that has been devoted to adorning cigar bands and boxes. The world's leading vitologist is a man by the name of Dr. Orlando Arteaga, president of the Cuban Vitolphilic Association. Is this, someone might ask, the most profound piece of information Schall ever learned? Well, of course not, but if I ever happen to meet Fidel Castro or some other cigar aficionado, I will have something to talk about. It puts a new light on the cigar, so to speak, to realize that such intricate work goes into decorating the band and box.

For a while, as a child, I used to do something equally useless as pursuing vitolas: I collected matchboxes and folders. The same principle of curiosity is involved. I recall learning a lot about geography from them. Most matchboxes give the address and city of whatever they are advertising. Somehow (I lived in Iowa as a boy), I once obtained a black matchbox from the Palmer House in Chicago, a hotel that was supposed to be, at the time, a pretty classy place and a rare matchbox. In later years, I went to a conference at the Palmer House and felt at home there because of that matchbox. The point here is that we can learn all about vitolas and all about matchboxes, and it won't hurt our brains a bit. In general, it is a good thing just to have a hobby that enables us to learn all about something, be it tabby cats, the batting averages of the Chicago Cubs starters, or the number of minnows in an average bass lake.

Matchboxes and vitolas aside, books will always remain, even in our paperless world, the basis of our learning and remembering. This is not to downplay the value and scope of the Internet or other electronic materials; I know we can find all the dialogues of Plato on some Web site, not to mention on CDs. However, reading a book, rereading a book, possessing a book, surrounding oneself with books, it seems to me, will always remain fundamental to in-depth learning, particularly of the highest things. A book we have read remains there for us to pick up again. It is ours; no one else has read, or perhaps marked it, as we have.

I once heard a TV interview with Shelby Foote, the great Civil War historian. He spoke of how he could only work within the surroundings of his own books, in his own home. This is probably true for many of us. When considering any future home we might rent, build, or buy, or any place in which we might work, we should be sure to provide adequate space for books, our own books, books we ourselves have obtained, read, marked, taken notes from, and put comments in.

Nothing is more disconcerting, it seems to me, than to enter a home or an apartment in which there are no books and no place for books, no sign that a book has ever been there. It always seems like a kind of desecration to me, even though I am perfectly aware that bookless people can also be saved, even that they often have much practical wisdom, something Aristotle himself recognized. I know that there are libraries from which we can borrow for a time a book we may not own. We are blessed to live in a time of relatively cheap books. Ultimately, no doubt, the important thing is what is in our head, not what is on a printed page on our shelves, even when they contain our own books. Nor do we have to replicate the New York City Public Library in our own homes. Still, most of us would benefit from having at least a couple hundred books, probably more, surrounding us. I am sure that by judicious use of sales and used-book and online stores, anyone can gather together a very respectable basic library, probably for less than a thousand dollars. With a little enterprise, one can find in a used bookstore or online the *Basic Works of Aristotle* or the *Lives of Plutarch* for less than twenty dollars. When stretched out over time and compared, say, to the cumulative price of supplies for a heavy smoker, or a week's stay in Paris or Tokyo, or a season ticket to one's favorite NFL team, the cost of books is not too bad. My point is merely that whether or not we have good books around us is not so much a question of cost as it is a question of what we do with our available money, with how we judge the comparative worth of things.

Remember, the important thing about a book is to know what it says. It is a living path to an author who is not here, who may in fact have lived centuries earlier, but who can still teach us. I once wrote an essay titled "On the Mystery of Teachers I Have Never Met," an account of the extraordinary fact that authors and thinkers long dead are still alive when we read them, are still able to instruct.[3] Books, as Plato said, are never as good as conversation, as direct encounters with actual men and women. But the very structure of our lives in time and space, though it may deprive us of their presence, does not deprive us of knowledge of those who lived before or away from us. So read intelligently. St. Paul says to "pray ceaselessly." I think we ought also to read ceaselessly. Reading, indeed, can itself be a form of prayer.

I have an old cartoon from Johnny Hart's *Wizard of Id* (April 16, 1969). In it, its hero, the little King, is sitting on his elegantly draped throne. Beside him is an official armored Page. The King commands him to "post this proclamation in the village square." In the next scene, the dutiful Page is seen in the square pounding the nails to hang up the proclamation, which ominously decrees: "'Henceforth, reading will be considered a crime against the state,' Signed, 'King.'" In the third panel, a rather pedestrian-looking citizen is seen hunched over reading the sign, while over his shoulder the Page is watching, even testing him. The Page inquires of the citizen, "What do you think of the King's proclamation?" The citizen faces about to the Page and answers in all shrewdness, "What proclamation?" Which is to say, the important thing is not to read, but to understand.

III

The first books I remember reading were probably from junior high school days, though I may well have read books of some sort earlier. I was not much read to or exposed to books. I did not know classic children's books, for example, some of which I have read as an adult (a most worthy enterprise). This neglect of books is probably due in part to the fact that my own mother died when I was nine. The point I make here is not to lament what I did not read, but to emphasize Johnson's idea that we ought to have an "eager desire for instruction," a desire simply to know. This desire, after all, is very Aristotelian—not that he "invented" it, but he pointed it out. For it was Aristotle who told us, in the beginning of his great *Metaphysics* (another book we should know about, possess, and read), that what incites us to know, to exercise this "eager desire for instruction," is simply "wonder"—not fear, or pleasure, or the lack of something (982b10–15). We just want to know. When we have all else, we will still want to know and to know more. This is the truth about us.

It makes no earthly difference, for example, for me to know what vitolphilia means, and yet I am glad to know it. I am delighted that I had something on my desk, just sitting around, that could tell me its meaning. Without it, as Johnson implied, I probably never would have bothered to look it up. The word is not, in fact, in my *Random House College Dictionary.* I also checked that huge and famous work, the *Oxford English Dictionary,* but in the miniaturized two-volume edition that has to be read with a magnifying glass, the word vitolphilia was not there either, much to my surprise. But vitola is a Spanish word, and it was in the Spanish dictionary I consulted.

I was in high school during World War II. I do not remember much of what I read at that time, but I distinctly recall one day finding in the local public library a book written by none other than the infamous Josef Stalin himself. So I decided to read it. It was a heavy tome, needless to say—Josef Stalin was not a humorist. I remember that the English editor of the book had put in footnotes about the number of Russians in concentration camps. But this warning made little impact on me at the time. I was evidently rather vain about the fact that I had managed to read such a book at all. I remember, much to her horror, praising this book to the mother of a young lady I was seeing at the time. Stalin, at that period, was in fact considered an ally of our country. In the book, he made what seemed to me to be almost a poetic case for his system—the only kind, I see now, that could possibly have been made for it. At the time, I really had little experience to know how properly to weigh what Stalin was saying against the truth. In retrospect, this experience was a good lesson, one confirmed by Aristotle himself, who warned that the young are not particularly adept students of political things (1095a2–5).

There are two other things I remember about the time before I was twenty and entered the Jesuit order, a move that subsequently provided me with a lot of time for catching up on my neglected reading. The first recollection is that my father had several novels by the English writers Owen Francis Dudley and Msgr. Robert Hugh Benson. These were, as I recall, rather apocalyptic tales, not unlike the more recent ones written by the Canadian novelist Michael O'Brien (*Father Elijah, Strangers and*

Sojourners, The Plague Journal, installations in a series of six novels O'Brien collectively titles *Children of the Last Days).* One of Dudley's titles was *The Shadow on the Earth* (1928). I must have read it during high school. I recall being quite frightened by it. Though Benson's *Lord of the World* was also on the side of the gods, it was, as I recall, quite alarming to read. In retrospect, I think the most frightening book that I ever read was the third of C. S. Lewis's Space Trilogy, *That Hideous Strength,* but *The Shadow on the Earth* was unnerving in the same way, in that it presented an unflinching recognition of the power of evil in the world, something probably worth being aware of, even in high school.

The other experience that I recall with regard to books came when I was in the army. At the time I was stationed at the Engineer School at Fort Belvoir, down the Potomac in Virginia, or maybe it was up in Camp Kilmer in New Jersey. World War II was just over, so there was no real pressure on troops. We had time to go to the post library. Once inside, I gazed perplexedly at the stacks and stacks of books. By that time, I had had a semester of college at the University of Santa Clara and was familiar with the Varsi Library there. But what sticks in my mind about the army library was the awareness that I did not know what to read, what to look for, or what was worth reading. Stacks of books are nothing if we have no idea how to choose among them. I suppose someone could go into a library and start with the first shelf and try to read to the end, A to Z in the Library of Congress system, but that would be both impossible and impractical. No one would ever, in a single lifetime, get beyond section "A" in any good-sized library.

But somehow out of all those books in the post library I selected and read a novel by Aldous Huxley. I think it was called *Chrome Yellow,* or something like that. It was unfortunately not *Brave New World,* a book that might have served to put Josef Stalin in some context. In fact, *Brave New World,* as my friend Jerome Hanus at American University has told me, is an extremely good book for students of today to read. It is rather accurate in its depiction of what would happen to our culture if we embraced certain modern principles in genetics and politics, principles that we evidently did embrace. But my point here is to emphasize this vivid sense of wanting to read but having no guidance, no clue about what is worth reading or how one would go about finding it.

This graphic experience of not knowing what to read, I think, lies at the origin of that tendency I have of giving students good, brief bibliographical lists of what to read. "Schall's Twenty Books to Keep Sane By," listed in my book *A Student's Guide to Liberal Learning*, or "Twenty Books That Tell the Truth," included in *On the Unseriousness of Human Affairs*, are merely recent manifestations of this peculiar tendency. In fact, the first appendix to this very book contains a list that I call "Schall's Twenty Books That Awaken the Mind."

IV

It is my experience that many of the most wonderful books are not read simply because the average student has not heard of them. Several years ago, I was teaching a class on Aquinas. Among the books assigned for the course was Chesterton's *St. Thomas Aquinas*, one of the most remarkable books ever written. After the semester, a student told me that he had had the book sitting on his desk after he had purchased it. Now and again, before it was actually assigned, he would, out of curiosity, read a page or two from it. He could not believe what a wonderful book it was. He wanted to know why no one had ever told him about Chesterton. I did not bother to point out that someone had.

I do think in retrospect, however, that reading almost anything, as Johnson said, gets us started. There is a very useful autobiography of the western novelist Louis L'Amour called *The Education of a Wandering Man*. In it, he recounts how he began to read and collect books, and how he gradually began to specialize mostly on his own. He acquired books about western America and all aspects of its settlement and geography. In this "wayfaring" book, L'Amour simply listed year by year the books that he read, along with a guide about how to find the time to read. The fact is, he makes clear, plenty of reading time exists if we will just rely on our own self-discipline, and more especially, if we will feed our desire to know.

Most people, moreover, have heard something of what are called the "great books," or the canon of books that we ought—or, according to some, ought not—to read. We need to realize that a great number of the best writers whom we most need to read have long been dead. Do not think that something is good merely because it is new or faddish. We will also find that those who are called the "great thinkers" contradict each other. It is easy, perhaps inevitable, for the study of the great books, if not accompanied by careful intellectual formation, to lead one into relativism or skepticism, though this is not a reason not to read them. Few of the really great thinkers were themselves skeptics. Indeed, the intellectual refutation of skepticism is almost the first serious step anyone needs to take to test the validity of his own mind and thinking powers. "Is it true that there is no truth?" remains the first test of mind, the first inkling we have that the principle of contradiction, that very basic intellectual tool, is operative in our own souls even when we try to deny it.

V

We need to surround ourselves with books because we are and ought to be curious about reality, about *what is*. The universe is not of our own making. Yet it is all right for us to be what we are, because the universe is potentially ours through our knowledge. In knowing, we become the other, become what we are not, as Aquinas taught. But in doing so, in coming to know, we do not change what it is that we know. We change ourselves. Our very intellectual being is intended to become what, in the beginning, we are not. This is the drama of our intellectual life, the life of our mind. We should spend our time on the highest things, Aristotle tells us, even though we may be able to grasp only a bit of them, even though it takes our whole lifetime (1177b31–1178a2).

In Mel Lazarus's cartoon series *Miss Peach* (January 7, 1968), we are placed in Miss Peach's kindergarten with Francine and Ira at their desks. Francine is rather uppity to the slower Ira. She is, to recall Johnson's point, surrounded by books. In fact, leafing through a book, she complains, "I read this book before. I have read them all." We next see that she is sitting behind Ira, who is reading his own book. Francine continues to elaborate: "(Sigh!) Sometimes I get the feeling that everything in the world has been said." Ira continues to endure her ongoing monologue: "All the philosophy, all the historical reflections, all the statements and observations have been made." He finally turns back to look at her over his shoulder, as she continues: "All the comments about society, life, the future, science, love, religion."

At this point, Francine becomes rather scolding to Ira, who merely raises his eyebrows. She charges with considerable eloquence: "All the words have been spoken, all the lines read, all the thoughts thought, all the ideas voiced, all the questions asked, all the remarks remarked, all the words worded, etc." Finally Francine asks a bleary-eyed, verbally shell-shocked Ira, "Do you feel that everything in the world has been said?" At last, Ira replies, "Yes, this afternoon, by you."

We cannot, of course, help but be amused by such a scene. We are aware of the passage in Ecclesiastes saying that indeed "there is nothing new under the sun" (2:9). And we are also aware that for each of us, everything is new. We begin our intellectual lives with minds that we did not give ourselves, with minds that have nothing in them until we begin to wonder, begin to know. Ira's witty reply about all things being said that afternoon by Francine reminds us of the limits of our pretensions to know, of the danger of pride that faces us constantly. Pride tells us, erroneously, that we already know enough, when we know that we do not know all things that can be known, including the highest things.

One of the books that we must have in our library is Augustine's *Confessions*, a book that, perhaps better than any other, accounts for the restlessness we cannot help but feel in our own souls concerning why we are here and what we are about. We are not only supposed to wonder about the highest things, but we are restless until we find them. As a very gifted but undisciplined young man of eighteen or nineteen, Augustine tells us, he came across a dialogue of Cicero (the *Hortensius*, now lost) written half a millennium earlier (*Confessions*, III, 4). He read this dialogue and it changed his life. He decided to pursue the truth. However, it still took Augustine a long time to figure things out. The young Augustine is still greatly attractive to us because he literally tried everything.

What the young Augustine still teaches us, something that is found in another way in Plato and Aristotle, is that our "restless hearts" lead us to seek—lead us indeed to find—but, we are nevertheless required to place things in order so that we do not call what is true or what is good what is not so. Having around us Augustine and Plato, Aquinas and Aristotle, Samuel Johnson and Chesterton, I think, will most surely and most quickly lead us to those things for which we have books in the first place, not to the books themselves, but to what is true, to what, as I like to say, makes sense—makes ultimate sense.

In the end, we should be careful when we read Stalin at fifteen or Cicero's *Hortensius* at nineteen. Both call us out of ourselves to a world we must judge. Though not all the "remarks are remarked," nor all "the words are worded," we still wonder and have restless hearts. Vitolphilia may not be a disease, but we can know what it is only if we have the right books surrounding us.

Tell me what you read and I will tell you what you are. In any intellectual life, books and the books we have around us do not just indicate where we started or where we have ended, but how we got there and why we did not go somewhere else or by some other path. They ground and provoke our inclination to know. Books and the intellectual life go together, provided we always remember that it is the books that are for the life of the mind and not the other way around.

This is why Sertillanges and Louis L'Amour, indeed, why Augustine and Aquinas, Johnson and Josef Pieper tell us that what comes first is the knowing. It is a terrible thing to go into a library and have no idea what to read, even when we know how to read. But the very realization of not knowing can exhilarate us too. After all, it is a great thing one morning to wake up and know that we want to know anything and everything. For we are, by nature, as the medieval writers said, *capax omnium*, capable of knowing all things.

Chapter III

Artes Liberales—THE LIBERAL ARTS

"Because," I said, "the free man ought not to learn any
study slavishly. Forced labors performed by the body
don't make the body any worse, but no forced study
abides in a soul."
   —Plato, *The Republic*

That there is to be education in music in such a way
that they will participate in the works [of music], therefore, is evident. What is appropriate and inappropriate
for different ages is not difficult to define and resolve, in
response to those who assert that the concern is a vulgar
one. In the first place, since one should share in the works
for the sake of judging, on this account they should practice the works when they are young, and when they become older leave off the works, and be able to judge the
noble things and to enjoy [them] in correct fashion
through the learning that occurred in their youth.
   —Aristotle, *Politics*

But in an orator we demand the acuteness of a logician,
the profundity of a philosopher, the diction virtually of a
poet, the memory of a lawyer, the voice of a performer in
tragic drama, the gestures, you might almost say, of an
actor at the very top of his profession.
   —Cicero, *On the Orator*

The Life of the Mind

I

The question of a proper education follows the question of what to read. The two, reading and education, are clearly related, though which comes first can well be disputed. In this chapter, I want to recall the familiar notion of the "liberal arts," those studies, those disciplines which, on going through them, enable us better to see what is there. The liberal arts are not one person's invention, but rather represent the collected wisdom of many generations and nations. We should recognize, from the beginning, that these "freeing" or "liberal" arts are not simply a body of books to read, but a way of life enabling us to be free enough to know the truth of things. When we do know something "for its own sake," we also know its truth or falsity; otherwise we do not really know it. It seems well, then, to take a further look at these famous "freeing arts."

II

In the *Crito* of Plato, we read that, during the month Socrates spent in jail awaiting the return of the sacrificial ship that would occasion his execution, Crito indicated that, from his personal wealth, he could easily provide a bribe to enable Socrates to escape. No one, even those who found him guilty as charged, really wanted Socrates to die. Besides, Crito, a rich friend of Socrates, would seem cheap in the eyes of the city and of his friends if he did not come forth with bribe money to free Socrates. A convenient place to which Socrates might go in exile, Crito informs him, is Thessaly, famous for its barbarian ways. Socrates had already rejected the other alternative of going to Thebes, a civilized city.

Socrates would not betray his vocation by ceasing to philosophize so that he could remain alive in Athens, the cultured city that Pericles had called the freest of all free cities in Greece. But Socrates rejected going to Thessaly because, in such a society, he would have no one with whom to talk. Philosophy exists in conversation. The barbarian king would, of course, know of the big-city fame of Socrates, the philosopher. He would have asked him to his court to perform some amazing feat to impress his retainers. Kings often found hapless philosophers amusing, while philosophers were known to have talked with, and even to have educated, kings.

Yet, for Socrates to be Socrates the philosopher, he would need to engage in conversation, in dialectic. Such dialectic required someone genuinely interested in the higher things. Socrates preferred audiences that consisted of those who had a deep desire to know. He only undertook to deliver monologues before corrupt, smooth politicians like Callicles in the *Gorgias*. Callicles refused further to engage Socrates in conversation lest he (Callicles) have to question his own political life and its supposedly unlimited freedom to do whatever he wanted. As he tells us, he had gone to college in his youth. Still, the young tyrant, by his own admission, had rejected the principles of liberal education. He ceased to be interested in all academic nonsense when he went into the active life of politics. Likewise, Thessaly's barbarian king was not liberally educated. Callicles lacked virtue, while the barbarian king lacked culture.

The barbarians in Thessaly, then, though worthy enough in their own ways, were not prepared systematically to examine their daily lives, the civic purpose that Socrates appointed to himself in *The Apology*. The barbarians would not have understood the point of such an "examined life." They were not "free" to know that they did not know. Socrates, who knew that he did not know, had to remain a private citizen even in Athens, lest he be eliminated sooner. Still, his whole life was engaged in conversations that could only take place in a city, albeit a disordered city, a democracy wherein freedom simply meant doing and saying whatever one wanted with no concern about its truth or effect. In this city, philosophers and fools were not easily separated because no principle of distinction was allowed or even thought to exist.

But in Athens, nevertheless, philosophic *eros* might have some chance of attracting the souls of potential philosophers, those who had not yet decided how they would live their lives. Though philosophy was not necessarily or fully at home in any existing city, including Athens, philosophers had to live in some place where they would not be killed, however much their being executed might confirm their philosophic vocations before the world. The cities in speech that they left us were designed to free us from actual cities even while living in them. To have no articulated "city" in one's soul is the essence of an unfree man. To have one, placed there by argument, is to be liberally educated.[1]

Likewise, in the New Testament, we read that Pilate, Christ's Roman judge, hears that Christ is from Galilee, a place outside of Pilate's immediate jurisdiction. In Galilee, the Romans had set up Herod, a puppet king. Pilate, who knew this whole business of executing Christ was likely to be messy, was delighted with the jurisdictional excuse that to try Christ was beyond his legal authority. So he packs him off to Herod's court for further judgment. Herod was shrewd. He had, of course, heard of this Jesus and was anxious to look him over. Like the barbarian king in Thessaly, Herod too wanted Christ to be on stage. We can imagine the scene when Christ is brought before Herod's court. Everyone is there, expecting some feat, perhaps some miracle, which many had heard Christ performed. It would give those at court something to talk about.

But, before Herod, Christ remains in complete silence. He will not "perform." He found nothing genuine in Herod, no way to reach his soul. Herod evidently was sensitive enough to get the point, so he returned Christ to Pilate. The Gospel of Luke notes that up until that time, Herod and Pilate, neither of whom was the absolute worst of men, were not on intimate terms, but now they became "friends." They both experienced this Christ, silent before them, refusing to respond to their falseness. Theirs was a friendship of complicity, of responsible men mutually rejecting their responsibilities in order to find pleasant consolation in their lethal jurisdictional game. If we are liberally educated, we cannot help but view this "friendship" against the classical concept of friendship as discussed by Plato, Aristotle, and Cicero.

We have here, to recall a phrase that Leo Strauss made famous, both "Jerusalem and Athens."[2] That is, we have the two origins of our

culture, the Greek heritage and the revelational response to its brood-
ing questions to itself. And these origins belong together, however
different each is. What is known as patristic and medieval thought is
designed to explain how this relationship is possible, how the best in
Athens can be seen as related to revelation and its unique terms. The
understanding of this relationship is what Chesterton once called "the
keenest of intellectual pleasures."[3] What is known as "modern" thought
is largely the attempt to solve the classical human questions without
recourse to either tradition.[4] Any adequate concept of "liberal arts" and
"liberal education" would, to be intellectually complete and honest,
have to attend to the Greek and Roman classical traditions, to the He-
brew and Christian revelation, to the patristic and medieval experience, and finally to modern claims, especially those arising from science and politics, even when they claim to be "autonomous." Students
who read Plato, Aristotle, St. Paul, and St. Augustine often are struck
to find themselves brought more up-to-date, in a way, than when they
read the *New York Times* or the latest textbook. The former sources
possess a freedom and an intelligence that the latter somehow lack.

III

We are familiar with colleges that describe themselves as "liberal arts"
colleges. We are also familiar with the distinction between things liberal and things servile. Work is sometimes designated, even in the Catholic Church, as "servile," something to avoid on Sundays. Certain disciplines, particularly what is known from Aristotle as "metaphysics," are
called freeing subjects. Such a "liberal" discipline is undertaken "for its
own sake," that is, the purpose of the knowledge gained is not to "do"
anything with it. Just to "know" something is itself a pleasure, even if
often we must learn to enjoy it. The "useful" crafts and disciplines,
even medicine and in their way art and law, are designed to "produce"
or "make" something. The work, though worthy in itself, is "for" something else. The hammer, though it may be in itself an artifact with

ornate carvings, is first intended to pound nails. To know how to make, decorate, and use a hammer is a craft, a realized relation between mind and reality.

The notion of "slavery," in which someone was designated to perform "servile" work or labor, did not initially refer to something wrong with the slave. Rather, it meant that something was wrong with the work he was forced to perform, because it had to be done for the very existence of human life, however droll. No one was willing voluntarily to do it. In the book of Exodus, we read: "[The Israelites] were made to work in gangs with officers set over them, to break their spirit with heavy labor. So [the Egyptians] treated their Israelite slaves with ruthless severity" (1:11–14). In short, they made use of them as slaves in every kind of hard labor. Such slavery, caused by conquest or other political means, did not imply anything about the slaves themselves. Roman professors were sometimes Greek slaves.

The so-called "natural" slave, strictly speaking, was, unlike the captive slave, someone who was not *causa sui*, or responsible for his own acts. Such a person had some real and objective defect in body or mind that could not be remedied. He could not rule himself but rather had to be ruled for his own good by another, be it a family or the state. Aristotle said, however, that if we could invent certain moving statues, perhaps it would be possible someday to make machines that would do much of the servile work that slaves were called to do, like weaving or pounding (1253b34–36). Such invention is indeed what eventually did happen in what came to be called the Industrial Revolution.

Much of the freedom from toil we experience in the modern world is because we have mechanical or technological "slaves" to do the work that is degrading for human beings to perform. Anyone who spends his time engaged in deadening or purposeless work, whether by coercion or by choice, would be considered, by the Greeks, to be a slave, however much we dislike that word. Moreover, as Yves Simon once remarked, if we contracted to pay a man a very high wage to dig a ditch six-by-six-by-six and then to fill it up again, only to begin the task once more, the man would soon go mad from this purposeless existence. Modern economics has shown ways for the drudgery of labor to be performed with dignity and profit by free citizens. If one thinks for instance, of modern sewage and waste management systems, we see how the work formerly forced on slaves can be carried out in another, more human, way.

The main Christian commentary about this situation was first not to deny that there was back-breaking work to be done, but rather, to affirm that the one who did it could nevertheless save his soul, that is, reach the highest things. Likewise, if work needed to be done, even if it was drudgery, it usually had a worthy purpose, no matter how difficult or boring. It might be regarded as a service to the poor, or to those who needed it, without which life could not go on. Even with adequate machinery, as modern totalitarian regimes have proved, without these two latter notions of personal salvation and objective service, legal slavery might never have been eliminated. Without them, slavery will no doubt return in some form or other. The worker has his dignity; the work has its purpose, but still there are things "for their own sake" that are not drudgery nor directly the Beatific Vision. The order of things to be known and done in the world remains a worthy project even if we may, on occasion, save our souls without them. This too is part of revelation.

Sundry machines and devices, from water wheels to computers and spacecraft, have been invented to do many of the tasks that were once considered inhuman and toilsome. We end up with what is called "free time." Our problem is what to do with it.

Is this time we now have left over merely "pastime"? Or are there things to be done that are not merely "useful"? This is the issue that Plato and Aristotle in ancient times, and Josef Pieper in modern times, have made famous under the notion of *skole*, or leisure.[5] Ancient cities were criticized because they used slaves to do servile work so that at least a few could be free enough to pursue other, more noble things. Modern cities are often criticized because they are full of people with free time that is frittered away on frivolous things. But the fact of free time is a good thing.

In a famous passage in the second book of *The Republic*, in the city he is building in speech, Socrates sketched a city with a sufficiency of worldly goods and indeed with an abundance of luxurious goods, all of which have come forth because of a demand caused by unlimited desire. Glaucon bitingly called this abundant economy "a city of pigs." That is, it was a city whose inhabitants had no higher goals than staying alive and being confident. Glaucon was aware that what was most important about human life had not yet even been discussed in the city in speech. In the classical sense of the term, the "liberal arts" have to do with these things which exist in the midst of or beyond abundance. Of course, this does not deny that the intellectual and productive efforts to make this abundance come to pass—the free market, the rules of justice and law, the value of work—are also, in their own ways, freeing and noble ones.

IV

"The liberal arts" have a history. The Greek and Roman experiences remain in some sense normative. To be free, we must carefully continue to study them. That is, the attentive reading of the Greek and Roman philosophical, literary, historical, and political traditions begins and continues a reflection into the heart of things that cannot be duplicated as easily or as elegantly by any other tradition. This is, in large part, because the Greeks and Romans regarded themselves as addressing mankind as such, however proud they were to be Greek or Roman. Metaphysics was not "Greek" metaphysics, but "metaphysics." Existing cities were Roman or Greek; political philosophy related to all cities. The principles of "oratory" were not Roman, but universal.

This tradition is worthy in itself. It is also worthy because subsequent traditions and cultures grew from this classical heritage. They commented on it, rewrote it, and even at times objected to it. The initial sources were enriched by the later ones. The end did not forget the beginning, nor did the beginning remain sterile to the end. It was not an accident that Cicero, as he tells us in his *De Officiis* ("On Duties"), sent his son, however unworthy, to Athens to study. Nor was it an accident that Augustine, as he tells us in *The Confessions*, decided, as a brash young man, to become a philosopher because of a now lost Ciceronian dialogue. Likewise, it is not surprising that Augustine's major work is titled *The City of God*, both because two Psalms speak of such a city (numbers 46 and 87) and because Plato wrote *The Republic*. We cannot read Augustine without, at the same time, reading the Greeks, the Romans, the Hebrews, and the Christians. Augustine was a man of "liberal learning," who even wrote a dialogue featuring his own son titled *De Magistro* ("On the Teacher"). Augustine still teaches us, but only if we let him.

One of the men most responsible for what are known as "great books programs," themselves designed as efforts to "save" liberal education, was Mortimer Adler.[6] "The liberal arts are traditionally intended to develop the faculties of the human mind, those powers of intelligence and imagination without which no intellectual work can be accomplished," Adler wrote:

Liberal education is not tied to certain academic subjects, such as philosophy, history, literature, music, art and other so-called "humanities." In the liberal-arts tradition, scientific disciplines, such as mathematics and physics, are considered equally liberal, that is, equally able to develop the powers of the mind. The liberal-arts tradition goes back to the medieval curriculum. It consisted of two parts. The first part, trivium, comprised grammar, rhetoric, and logic. It taught the arts of reading and writing, of listening and speaking, and of sound thinking. The other part, the quadrivium, consisted of arithmetic, geometry, astronomy, and music (not audible music, but music conceived as a mathematical science). It taught the arts of observation, calculation, and measurement, how to apprehend the quantitative aspect of things. Nowadays, of course, we would add many more sciences, natural and social. This is just what has been done in the various modern attempts to renew liberal education.[7]

The medieval trivium and quadrivium, indicated the place where three roads (*tres viae*) or four roads (*quatro viae*) of knowledge crossed in the same person. The quadrivium, in particular, had to do with numbers—arithmetic meant "number in itself," geometry meant "number in space," music meant "number in time," and astronomy meant "number in space and time."[8] Without preparation in such disciplines, thought the medievals, we lack the intellectual tools to understand the world. Each discipline was worthy of study in itself, but once all were acquired, the student was "free" to stand before all things as a whole, both to know and to act. Hence the notion associated with "liberal arts" was "universal" or "general."

V

In the classical medieval tradition, to be a complete human being, there were things worth doing and knowing. Man was an animal who freely needed to complete himself to be what he was intended to be. But this "self-completion" was not considered to be, though it could be, an act of pride or autonomy, that is, an act that made man the cause of the distinction in things. The fact that man had to "complete" himself in order to be what he was intended to be was itself a challenge in one's own soul. It paid deference to one's own initiative and freedom.

Education, moreover, was not a "thing." The word *educere* means to bring forth, or to complete something already begun by the very fact that one is a human being. We do not "make ourselves" to be human beings, as Aristotle constantly affirmed, though we do make ourselves to be good or bad human beings, complete or incomplete human beings. Yet, the freedom to become bad or evil is itself a kind of slavery, since it deflects us from our proper end. This is why the path to freedom in the classical tradition has always been pictured as one consisting of acquiring virtues and avoiding corresponding vices.

To the ancients, the human mind itself had its own proper functioning; once it was "free" to know, then it was supposed to go ahead and know. This was the real adventure. The mind was *capax omnium*, capable of knowing all the things it did not itself make or create. Aristotle remarked that there is a proper pleasure attached to every human activity, including the activities of thinking and knowing, as well as sensing, willing, doing, and making. It would not be wrong to describe "liberal education" as the effort to experience the proper pleasure due to knowing, according to what they are, *all the things that are*—seeing, tasting, listening, touching, smelling, remembering, imagining, knowing, thinking, and believing. "To be learning something is the greatest of pleasures," Aristotle remarked in a surprisingly open phrase, "not only to the philosopher but to the rest of mankind, however small their capacity" (148b13–15). But since we can choose disorder, since we can reject the kind of being we ought to be, it is quite possible to be illiberally educated; indeed it is possible to acquire and practice vices instead of virtues while knowing what both are. What would someone who does not acquire the proper formation of his soul look like?

We are fortunate to have excellent descriptions of the illiberally educated man. Let me cite two portrayals—one from Plato and one from the English novelist Evelyn Waugh. In each of these descriptions, we find pictured a man who can certainly read and write, who is active in public, and who, no doubt, thinks he is properly educated. But in each description, it is clear that the person portrayed lacks the very order of soul and mind that would enable us to call him "free" and judicious in his relation to the highest things.

In the eighth book of *The Republic*, Plato describes the soul of the democratic man, the man who is "free," that is, the man with no order of principle in his soul. What is his day like? And why? How does he appear before others? This is Plato's graphic description.

"[H]e doesn't admit any word of truth into the guardhouse [of his soul], for if someone tells him that some pleasures belong to the fine and good desires and others to evil ones and that he must pursue and value the former and restrain and enslave the latter, he denies all this and declares that all pleasures are equal and must be valued equally." (Socrates)

"That is just what someone in that condition would say." (Adeimantus)

"And so he lives on, yielding day by day to the desire at hand. Sometimes he drinks heavily while listening to the flute; at other times, he drinks only water and is on a diet; sometimes he goes in for physical training; at other times, he's idle and neglects everything; and sometimes he even occupies himself with what he takes to be philosophy. He often engages in politics, leaping up from his seat and saying and doing whatever comes into his mind. If he happens to admire soldiers, he's carried in that direction, if money-making, in that one. There's neither order nor necessity in his life, but he calls it pleasant, free, and blessedly happy, and he follows it for as long as he lives." (Socrates, 561b–d)

It would be difficult to find a more blunt description of what a liberally educated man is not. Such is the man who thinks that his life is pleasant and free when it is, by any objective evaluation, just the opposite.

Each point of the young man's disordered soul needs emphasizing: on occasion he jogs to keep in shape. Next, however, he is found with a beer, lounging around mostly watching TV. One day, after seeing or hearing one, he desires to be a banker, the following day a soldier, the day after even a philosopher. He drinks heavily, then goes on a diet and drinks only water. He denies himself no pleasure, considers all pleasures equal whether they follow good or bad actions. In short, the man has no principle of order in his soul. He has no way to distinguish worthy and unworthy ways of life. Such a person is very dangerous both to himself and to his polity precisely because his soul is disordered by a lack of discipline and knowledge of what human life is about. Plato never tired of reminding the potential philosopher that the condition of his city ultimately depended on the condition of his soul. No political reform could ever be successful without personal reform. No one who did not understand this relationship could be "liberally" educated.

The second passage I should like to cite in this consideration of what no one would want to be, of how a faulty education fails to teach one the truth of things, including human things, comes from Evelyn Waugh's novel *Brideshead Revisited*. In the early part of World War II, Waugh had occasion to comment on the type of modern young man who comes into the army. He is clearly a young man of modern education and taste, a worthy successor to the democratic youth described by Plato. This young man's name is Hooper.

> Hooper was no romantic. He had not as a child ridden with Rupert's horse or sat among the camp fires at Xanthus-side; at the age when my eyes were dry to all save poetry—that stoic, red-skin interlude which our schools introduce between the fast flowing tears of the child and the man—Hooper had wept often, but never for Henry's speech on St. Crispin's Day, nor for the epitaph at Thermopylae. The history they taught him had few battles in it but, instead, a profusion of detail about humane legislation and recent industrial change. Gallipoli, Balaclava, Quebec, Lepanto, Bannockburn, Roncevales, and Marathon—these, and the Battle of the West where Arthur fell, and a hundred such names whose trumpet-notes, even now in my sere and lawless state, called to me irresistibly across the intervening years with all the clarity and strength of boyhood, sounded in vain to Hooper.[9]

Hooper evidently had a social science education, heavy on statistics and "facts." He did not know about the great events of history that ought to have filled his boyhood imagination. He was not liberally educated. He was not free.

In book four of Aristotle's *Ethics*, the word "liberal" initially had to do with material possessions. Aristotle saw that man, to be virtuous, needed a certain amount of material goods. He also understood that we reveal our souls by how we deal with the material goods, large and small, that we do have. The Greek word *elutheria* referred to that virtue by which we rule our material goods so that we can achieve our higher purposes by their proper use. The word is sometimes translated as "generosity" or "liberality." It has two aspects, the person with ordinary wealth and the person with immense wealth. Aristotle was not particularly worried that some people had more wealth than others. He recognized no "preferential option for the poor" and perhaps served them better because of it. Rather, he was concerned with how wealth was used. Liberality or generosity is a virtue precisely because it is designed to free us from ourselves, to allow us to see that what we possess is also shared with others not just for their good but for their enjoyment.

"Freedom to welcome truth, without hindrance on the part of our mind, certainly is a rare privilege," Yves Simon has written in a perceptive essay titled, "Freedom from the Self":

> That human freedom should be restricted in this high order of the mind's relation to truth is a moral and metaphysical disaster of the first magnitude. Knowing is the creature's best chance to overcome the law of nonbeing, the wretchedness inflicted upon it by the real diversity of "that which is" and "to be." A thing which is not God cannot *be* except at the cost of *not being what it is not.* It cannot be except by being deprived of indefinitely many forms and perfections. To this situation, knowledge, according to St. Thomas's words, is a remedy, inasmuch as every knowing subject is able to have, over and above

its own form, the forms of other things. This remedy is, so to say, complete in the case of intellectual knowledge, for intelligent beings can have the forms of all things and be all things spiritually, intentionally, transsubjectively, objectively.[10]

Freedom from the self is first required that we might have a freedom for others, a freedom to know *what is*.

We cannot be the kind of being we are unless we are not other things. Thus, it is all right to be what we are. Yet, what we are contains this mind with its *capax omnium*, with its capacity to know *all that is*. It is this exciting freedom to take into our souls what we are not, to take it in without changing or destroying what we take in, that constitutes the purpose of the liberal arts, which are designed to teach us how to be open to the various levels of being.[11]

VI

Donald Kagan has traced the various meanings that have been given to the term "liberal arts" or a "liberal education." Generally, the term has included the ideas 1) that knowledge is its own purpose, an end in itself, that it is good to know, 2) that liberty means having the virtues whereby we can rule ourselves, 3) that knowledge includes something useful, some worthy way of making one's way in the world, and 4) that this liberal learning has a political component, the ideal of living in a free society, of participating in ruling and being ruled.[12] The Roman notion of education was more practically oriented than the Greek classical view. The Romans stressed the capacity of speech, of eloquence. Aristotle had said in his *Rhetoric* that a man should be able to defend himself as well with his speech as he can with his arms.

The medieval university, having newly discovered Aristotle and being familiar with revelation and the classical heritage through the fathers of the church, considered that a liberal education dealt with already discovered things. The source of truth was God, both as known by reason and by revelation. Logic and dialectic studies seemed the best way to prepare oneself for grasping what is known. The medieval *summae* and curricula, while not neglecting practical things, attempted to organize all of what men knew into one orderly, interrelated whole.[13] The Renaissance notion of a liberal education was in part an effort to return to the ancients minus the addenda of revelation while minimizing the Greek notion of the contemplative life. There was a revival of the notion of the primacy of the city and its demands. The focus again became "this worldly." Finally, modern educators were more interested in what was not yet known. The "scientific method" stressed not what was revealed or what was previously learned or even what was useful for the city, but "new things." With the spread of the "scientific method" into all disciplines, including the liberal ones, with its implication of "progress," it was proposed that the secret to general education was at hand.

The modern university is "liberal" in the sense that it does not have any principle of order. No department or branch of knowledge seems to have any priority over the other. Each discipline has in common only what each discipline maintains about itself. In this context, it becomes almost impossible to have a "liberal education" in the classical sense. Not merely do the great books seem to contradict each other, but so do the "truths" that are taught in the various disciplines.[14] The primacy of relativism as the ground for democratic education seems to flow from the condition of modern knowledge, as it flowed from Aristotle's notion that "democracy" was based on that understanding of liberty which had no order other than that of its own choosing. Universities are perhaps useful as a place for the preparation of elite students who will, by a kind of aristocratic heritage, gain control of certain professions and offices in the economy and in politics. But they do not provide a genuine "liberal education." Not merely are the classics and revelation considered to be inadmissible as norms or canons for the education of all, but the sciences themselves never know what they might be in the future. The conclusion of this observation is not that there is no place for liberal learning, but that its place may not always, or even usually, be found in academic institutions.[15]

VII

We are, of course, reluctant to admit that the case for "liberal education," for "liberal arts," for the things that free us from slavery to the self and from being content with the merely useful is hopeless. Liberal education is not a "specialty." It is not what is called a "major." Rather, it is rooted in the kind of intellectual *eros* that we find in Plato, in the "wonder" that according to Aristotle stimulates all thought, in the drive to know what reoriented the life of the young Augustine when he read Cicero. This *eros* lies behind all we do, since all things are worth knowing. Jacques Maritain put the issue bluntly: "Great poets and thinkers are the foster-fathers of intelligence. Cut off from them, we are simply barbarians."[16] That we be not barbarians, that we be not cut off from the great poets and thinkers, is what it means to be "free," to know the *things that are.*

The liberal arts have something to do both with solitude and with the city. Cicero began the third part of his famous *De Officiis* ("On Duties") with these memorable words: "Publius Cornelius Scipio, the first of the family to be called Africanus, used to remark that he was never less idle than when he had nothing to do, and never less lonely than when he was by himself."[17] On the other hand, we feel the draw of the city in this passage from Boswell. He and Samuel Johnson had stayed overnight at St. Albans. The following day, March 29, 1776, Boswell writes, "I enjoyed the luxury of our approach to London, that metropolis which we both loved so much, for the high and varied intellectual pleasure which it furnishes."[18] Here we have the classic theme that there are genuine intellectual pleasures to be found in cities too. Of course, the reading and rereading of both Cicero and Boswell's *Life of Johnson* might of itself be considered a liberal education. There is more, but these are good beginnings, indeed good endings of such an enterprise. Great thinkers, no doubt, can be and have been in error; Aristotle, who knew Plato's worry that the poets could corrupt us, understood that the knowledge of error—even great error—is not something that we should reject knowing. It is part of being free. "We must, however, not only state the true view," Aristotle observed, "but also explain the false views, since an explanation of that promotes confidence. For when we have an apparently reasonable explanation of why a false view appears true, that makes us more confident of the true view." (*Ethics*, 1154a23–26). The history of error, the history of heresy (I think of Chesterton's *Heretics*), is as much a part of liberal education as is the history of truth. The reading of what is in fact error is also a way to keep sane. A considerable part of being intelligent and virtuous consists in knowing what it is to be unintelligent and vicious, especially in the graphic terms given to us by our literature.

Unless we understand the arguments against truth, we do not fully understand truth itself. And the arguments against truth can be very persuasive. Josef Cardinal Ratzinger, now Pope Benedict XVI, himself a man of genteel and liberal leaning, gave a good example of this awareness of how it is a part of being free to know where ideas lead. "The central problem of our time," he observed on October 6, 2001, at the Synod of Bishops in Rome, "is the emptying-out of the historical figure of Jesus. It begins with denying the virgin birth, then the resurrection becomes a spiritual event, then Christ's awareness of being the Son of God is denied, leaving Him only the words of a rabbi. Then the Eucharist falls, and becomes just a farewell dinner."

John Henry Newman, whose book *The Idea of a University* stands at the heart of any modern discussion of the liberal arts, made this point about the difference between liberal education and salvation:[19] no matter how valuable natural virtues are, they do not themselves guarantee supernatural excellence. The gentleman, while perhaps being exquisitely refined, can still lose his soul.[20] This is just another way of saying that man has a destiny higher than perfection in this world. Indeed, it implies that perfection even in this world is not complete without attention to man's ultimate purpose. Any education can stop short of attending to this higher purpose, but it does so at the cost of ignoring that what is true in this world always points us toward something higher.

Aristotle gave many hints that something more was "due" to human nature than has been given to it, though he was not quite sure what it was. "Such a (contemplative) life would be superior to the human level. For someone will live it not in so far as he is a human being, but in so far as he has some divine element in him." (*Ethics*, 1177b27– 28). This passage suggests why it may be "illiberal" not to include all that we can know of man in our "freeing" education of him. The best "natural" explanations of our condition as human beings seem to be aware that we are lacking something, not merely because of a certain "wickedness" of which even Aristotle was aware, but because nothing we find in our ordinary ways seems to satisfy us (*Politics*, 1267b1). This again is Augustine's realism.[21]

An education that does not include explanations and understandings of what we are fails to give us the necessary intellectual tools and information fully to explain us to ourselves. To explain man to himself is the central purpose of any form of liberal education. It is also, as John Paul II often said, the purpose of Christianity. Christian literature presupposes certain unanswered, often brilliant questions that had already occurred to the human mind before Christianity itself came into being. The liberally educated man knows these classic questions as they arise in any soul, including his own. A liberally educated Christian cannot understand his own revelation if he too does not know the force of these classic questions.

In conclusion, the liberal arts include the intellectual *eros* that is unsettled by not knowing what is true. If we read descriptions of this philosophic *eros* alongside the revelational proposition that *homo non proprie humanus sed superhumanus est*, we might at least come to suspect that this unsettlement is something put there from the beginning.[22] That is why to be free—that is, to be "liberally educated," to practice the truly "liberal arts"—is to be open to something that is not ourselves, and not made by ourselves. Mankind's story is more a drama of his receptivity than it is of his creativity, though it is that too.

The final word, I think, should belong to Aristotle, the man who made us most aware that there is an order in things. "For self-sufficiency and action do not depend on excess," he wrote in the *Ethics*, "and we can do fine actions even if we do not rule earth and sea; for even from moderate circumstances we can do the actions expressing virtue" (*Ethics*, 1179a2–6). Ordinary people can engage in actions that express virtue; they can know *what is*. The revelational side of this same principle is simply that everyone, king or pauper, can—with grace—save his own soul. If we combine these two principles, we have the essence of what it is to be free, free both to know what the world is like and to know our own destiny.

Chapter IV

ON TAKING CARE OF ONE'S OWN WISDOM

Boswell: "By associating with you, Sir, I am always getting an accession of wisdom. But perhaps a man, after
knowing his own character, the limited strength of his
own mind, should not be desirous of having too much
wisdom." Johnson: "Sir, be as wise as you can; let a man
be *aliis laetus, sapiens sibi.* You may be wise in your study
in the morning, and gay in company at a tavern in the
evening. Every man is to take care of his own wisdom
and his own virtue, without minding too much what
others think."
—Boswell, *Life of Johnson*

"For many of my years (perhaps twelve) had passed away
since my nineteenth, when, on the reading of Cicero's
Hortensius, I was roused to a desire for wisdom."
—St. Augustine, *The Confessions*

"The proper operation of man as man is to understand,
for by reason of this [understanding] he differs from all
other things."
—Thomas Aquinas, *Commentary on
Aristotle's* Metaphysics

I

The books we read, the liberal arts themselves, are ultimately designed to teach us to be wise—the highest of the virtues, as Aristotle tells us in the sixth book of his *Ethics*. Some things, when they happen right before our eyes, we obviously should be prepared to notice or appreciate. Or, to state this same principle in the opposite way, it is quite possible not to pay attention to the greatest things of human existence even when they happen right in front of us. Such is our fate.

In an old *Miss Peach* cartoon (to make this point of noticing and not noticing in still another way), we see Francine and her girlfriends listening to the radio. The evening news excitedly reports that "a flood is raging through the west side of town; the earthquake is beginning to rumble again."

In the next scene, Francine says, with some concern, "Say, I just realized that Arthur is over in that part of town." The girls, of course, do not think Arthur is overly swift. Arthur suddenly appears. They ask him, "Arthur, were you just over on the other side of town?" "Yes," he replies. "Really? Did you see the floods? And the earthquake?" Modestly, Arthur replies, "Oh, yes." "You did? Did you take pictures? Did you write everything down?" "No," Arthur admits.

To which incredible response, Francine says, "You didn't? Then did you at least remember it vividly?" "Can you tell us about it?" another girl asks. "Uh, not too well," Arthur confesses. This inattentiveness infuriates the girls. "What? You oaf! You were only right in the middle of the greatest natural disaster in years and you have absolutely no impressions of it?" The three girls turn their backs on a perplexed Arthur. "Fool!" "Ninny!" "Insensitive clod!" they yell. Arthur is next seen standing alone, somewhat puzzled. Finally, in the last scene, defending himself, he protests, "Nobody told me it was an experience."[1]

Some "experiences," the most important ones, we need not be told about. I suppose that is the real meaning of the brief citation from Aquinas, "the proper operation of man as man is to understand, for by reason of this [understanding] he differs from all other things." We are the beings whose distinguishing purpose, indeed whose distinguishing delight, is that we understand first what is not ourselves and, by that means, understand ourselves also. The first step is the consciousness that something has happened, not necessarily "the greatest natural disaster in years," but some real event, some experience.

II

In a famous scene in his *Confessions,* St. Augustine tells of going to the villa at Cassiciacum near Lake Como in Italy. He knew he had reached some kind of crisis, more of the will than of the intellect. He acknowledged, recalling his teenage decision arrived at after reading Cicero, that his purpose was to become "wise," but, he frankly admitted, "still I delayed to reject merely worldly happiness" (VIII, c. 7). Looking around for some way to resolve his inner difficulties, he at last went into the garden of the villa where, unexpectedly, he heard a voice of a child telling him to "take up the book and read it." He opened a book containing the letters of Paul. He took the first lines that chanced to meet his eyes to be prophetic in his personal life. They appeared to be directed specifically to him, at that particular time in his life. He was then in his early thirties.

The first words that Augustine saw were the following ones from Paul's Letter to the Romans: "Not in rioting and drunkenness, not in chambering and wantonness, not in strife and envying; but put on the Lord Jesus Christ, and make not provision for the flesh, to fulfil the lusts thereof" (13:13; VIII, c. 12). Naturally, since this passage contained a pretty accurate description of exactly what the young Augustine had been doing in recent years, he finally, if reluctantly, decided at their prompting to change his ways. He was, in Platonic terms, ready to "turn around," to face reality, often the most difficult task in life.

The reason I cite this passage from Augustine, to continue these considerations on what I call, in general, "liberal learning," is because I decided to use the same method of selection that Augustine used to find the passage from Romans. However, I used Boswell's *Life of Johnson* instead of the Epistle to the Romans, not that I have anything against Romans! Thus, I took out my battered old copy of Boswell, from, as we have seen, St. Peter's High School Library, St. Petersburg. I opened it up. The first words that I saw were those from the conversation between Boswell and Johnson about wisdom and one's own responsibility to attain it. This wisdom is, after all, the end of liberal learning.

The passage in Boswell, in fact, is rather strikingly parallel to the passage of Augustine wherein he tells us how the chance reading of a now lost dialogue of Cicero in a small town in northern Africa moved his very soul. From this chance encounter with Cicero, Augustine, as we saw earlier, desired to be a philosopher, nothing less. This "turning around" of the soul of Augustine, to use a Platonic phrase, was a momentous event in the history of mankind, as indeed were the writings of Cicero themselves. Something had changed in Augustine's soul, even though he had a long way to go. The main thing that prevented his becoming a philosopher sooner was the way he was living. There is a relation between how we live and what we see, between how we live and our willingness to affirm the truth. We want to concoct a philosophy to justify our chosen ways, rather than choose to rule ourselves according to a true and perennial philosophy.

In the case of Boswell, as we read in his *London and Continental Journals*, his youth was lived in a rather more riotous and even more "chambering" way than the young Augustine, who was at least faithful to his unnamed concubine while the relationship lasted. Still, not unlike Augustine with Ambrose, Boswell had found in Johnson someone of the stature even of a Socrates, and he knew it. Like Adeimantus and Glaucon on meeting Socrates in the Second Book of *The Republic*, Boswell knew that he must talk to the man as much as possible. Happily for us, he also recorded in his journals these conversations. The highest things can strike us when we are quite unprepared for them, even unworthy of them. But of course the highest things always have the potential of turning us around, if we choose to let them. We are not, by nature, self-enclosed, but "self-open" beings. Boswell frankly doubts his own resolution and his persistency in attaining wisdom. His mind, he thinks, only has a "limited strength." Johnson listens to these somewhat vain protestations. He does not accept their spirit, which is why Johnson is a great philosopher.

Instead, Johnson tells Boswell to be as wise as "he can." Just because we are not an Aristotle is no reason for us to do little or nothing with what we are given by nature. Each life is its own philosophic adventure aimed at finding the truth and living it. We should indeed, to recall Johnson's Latin phrase, *aliis laetus, sapiens sibi*, present a "happy face to others, but wisdom to ourselves." Johnson knew the difference between a study in the morning and a tavern in the evening. He was not disparaging the tavern, for the tavern, too, is a place of conversation, often profound, as any reader of Boswell soon learns. We are, however, to "take care of our own wisdom." It is only by the activity of our own minds, whereby we intentionally possess the universe, that wisdom may become ours. This knowing is why, again, Aristotle defines the human mind as that power by which we are capable of knowing all things.

Johnson has not, in telling us to "take care of our own wisdom," become a modern relativist who thinks that whatever we hold is by that fact alone "wisdom." Rather, he means that we are ultimately responsible for our own learning of what is true. We really do not want to affirm that just anything we happen to think is for that reason true. If everyone thought that, there could be no conversation, no quest, no truth. If we miss the excitement of truth itself, it is largely our own fault, even though most of us need the help of good habits and of good teachers, (sometimes alive but more often dead). We are not to be deflected from its pursuit by our own timidity or by the views of others. We should not "mind" what others think of our quest—provided that like Augustine, we are struck by the need to pursue philosophy in the first place.

This attention to wisdom means that we need in our souls a genuine philosophy, a genuine learning, if you will, that can enable us to seek, and yes, to know what is truly worthy of being known. Thus, recalling the examples of Augustine and Boswell, we must first hear in our souls a "call to be wise." I do not conceive this "call" as some sort of voice in the night whispering outside our window, "Be wise, Schall," even though something like that appears to have happened to Augustine and even to Paul and Socrates. But it is invariably manifested by an unsettlement in our souls, a sense that we are made to know, but we do not yet actually know.

When we are young, we generally learn that we have the "power" or "capacity" to know when we first have learned something. To make us aware of this knowing was the purpose of the exercise of the three fingers in Book Seven of *The Republic*, where we begin to see that long is not short, that one is not two, and that we can distinguish one thing from another. The more profound "experience"—to use Arthur's word—as described by Augustine and Boswell, comes later on, the sudden realization of what we do not know placed side-by-side with the suspicion that we can know the truth of things. As Plato said, we do not want to lie to our souls about the most important things, we do not want to lie to ourselves about *what is*—to others perhaps we sometimes do want to lie, but not to ourselves.

St. Thomas Aquinas records a famous phrase at the beginning of his *Commentary on Aristotle's Ethics*. It reads, *sapientis est ordinare*; "it is the task of the wise man to order things." I would suggest then that our first "call" to wisdom is this very unsettlement we find in our souls, when we begin to wonder whether things are ordered and, if so, how things are ordered. How is the world made? How is it that I am the kind of being that I am, a being who can ask such a question? The sort of experience that I am talking about here, I suspect, does not usually happen much before the age of nineteen or twenty. Plato warns us of confronting such philosophical things when we are too young. Even less do I think that we become wise at such an early age. It is no accident that tradition associates old age with wisdom. A "senate" literally means a chamber full of old, and therefore presumably wise, men—those who have learned. But this same tradition does not deny that, in practice, some senators are fools or corrupt, as Cicero reminded us in his famous speech "Against Verres." There are experiences that make us "wise before our time," but we prefer not to have them too soon.

III

I was once, while I was still in Rome, given a book by Gilbert Highet, the great professor of Latin at Columbia University. It was titled *Poets in a Landscape: Great Latin Poets in the Italy of Today*. My copy was first published in London in 1957 by Hamish Hamilton. The poets that Highet deals with are Catullus, Vergil, Propertius, Horace, Tibullus, Ovid, and Juvenal. Juvenal, whose full name was Decimus Junius Juvenalis, was born, evidently near a town called Roccaseca, or Dry Rock, during the reign of the Emperor Nero in about 60 A.D. The nearest large town to Roccaseca was Aquinum, itself not too far from Arpinum, where Cicero was born. Thus, Juvenal came from the same rugged area that was eleven hundred years later to give birth to Thomas Aquinas. Juvenal was a soldier, but he never made it to the high ranks of Roman society. At one point exiled to Egypt, he is famous for his satires; his poetry is full of personal disappointments.

Highet's elegant description of Juvenal has something touching and poignant about it. He broaches a theme that I have already hinted at—the relation of fame and wisdom. "When he started his career, he had no intention of becoming a poet," Highet informs us:

He wanted to be something much grander: an official of the Roman government. It was only when he failed of his first ambition that he turned to poetry. And even then he was a comparative failure—as judged by his own bold ambitions and his resounding challenge to rival poets. During his lifetime, his satires produced hardly any effect whatever. After his death, they were forgotten for nearly two hundred years. It would have astounded him, accustomed as he was to bitter disappointments and to ironic twists of destiny, to learn that centuries after he died the Romans would rediscover his poems.[2]

One of the abiding lessons of the history of thought is that the wise are not always, or even often, recognized in their own lifetimes. *Sic transit gloria mundi*. That is, there is a difference between fame and wisdom.

Yes, fame should go with wisdom, thought with act. What is worthy to be acknowledged should in fact be acknowledged. In one sense, the terribleness of the vice of envy consists precisely in knowing something or someone is worthy of honor, but refusing to acknowledge it. Envy is a much more dangerous vice than, say, greed, as it lies closer to the spirit, to our free will. Still, it remains the mark of wisdom to prefer truth to fame, to prefer obscurity to a publicity that is not based on truth, to recognize the dangers of vanity.

One of Juvenal's most famous satires is "On the Vanity of Human Ambition." It was translated by the great English poet John Dryden in 1693. "Tis plain from hence that what our vows request / Are hurtful things, or useless at the best, / Some ask for envied power: which public hate / Pursues, and hurries headlong to their fate: / Down go the titles: and the statue crowned / Is by base hands in the next river drowned." The theme of the vanity of human wishes or ambition, of course, reflects an awareness that our failed wishes, perhaps even our successes, point to another destiny.

It happens, of course, that Samuel Johnson, in January 1749, published his own "Vanity of Human Wishes" as an imitation of this same Tenth Satire of Juvenal. Just as Augustine could be stirred by Cicero, so Johnson could be moved by Juvenal. Boswell remarks that Johnson seems to have had all of Juvenal's *Satires* memorized. Though some thought this poem of Johnson rather heavy, Boswell himself acknowledged its greatness: "*The Vanity of Human Wishes* is, in the opinion of the best judges, as high an effort of ethick poetry as any language can shew. The instances of variety of disappointment are chosen so judiciously and painted so strongly, that, the moment they are read, they bring conviction to every thinking mind."[3] Indeed, the purpose of philosophy, as that of poetry in its own way, is to "bring conviction to every thinking mind." We do not read just to read. If in fact "books beget books," both in terms of writing and in terms of reading them, it is because through the book, through making it alive in our own minds and comparing it with reality itself, we arrive at knowledge and, we hope, wisdom.

If we seek wisdom from what we read, it is good to compare the conclusion of Juvenal's satire, with the statue of fame broken and tossed into the river, with Johnson's conclusion, which has room also for more than pagan resignation:

Yet when the sense of sacred presence fires,
And strong devotion to the skies aspires,
Pour forth thy fervours for a healthful mind,
Obedient passions, and a will resign'd;
For love, which scarce collective man can fill,
For patience, sovereign o'er transmuted ill;
For faith, which panting for a happier seat,
Counts death kind Nature's signal for retreat.
These goods for man the law of Heaven ordain,
These goods He grants, who grants the power to gain;
With these celestial wisdom calms the mind,
And makes the happiness she does not find.[4]

Here we see the difference between a Christian mind and a pagan one. The pagan mind is indeed "fired" by a "sacred presence." There is a "love" that "collective man" cannot fulfill. The mind does not find happiness, though it seeks it. What fame we have in our worldly experience seems to end when our monuments of fame lie broken in the river. The Christian, however, is given a "celestial wisdom" to calm his mind. This is what revelation is about. It does not forget the searches of the pagans or the vanities to which, like them, we are tempted. But it allows us to gaze in the river at the broken statues with a calm mind, knowing this world is not the end.

IV

In Plato's *Symposium*, one of the most famous of passages is that in which the handsome, brilliant, ambitious, and thoroughly corrupt Alcibiades appears. Of all the potential philosophers who appear in Plato's writings about Socrates, this young man was the one with the most potential. He was the most persuasive and charming, the one who, by betraying philosophy, did the most damage. In the end, he also betrayed his city. "How is this possible?" we might wonder. No greater description in all literature exists than these passages depicting the power of will and ambition to resist and reject wisdom, even when it is offered to us in its most attractive form, an attraction we, like Alcibiades, readily acknowledge.

Alcibiades grew up in the house of the great Pericles. He had heard some of the great orations that we may still read in Thucydides, who also records the subsequent ironic fate of this same Alcibiades in betraying both Athens and Sparta, even Persia. Alcibiades, in the *Symposium,* describes his admiration for great speeches. But none of them unsettle his soul like the conversations with Socrates, who at one time saved Alcibiades' life in battle. These other speakers "never upset me so deeply that my very own soul started protesting; that my life—*my* life!—was no better than the most miserable slave's" (215e). Socrates, however, makes Alcibiades think differently. "He makes it seem that my life isn't worth living!"

But Alcibiades will not let Socrates address him, or his soul. As he explains it to the other listeners at the Supper of Agathon, Socrates "always traps me, you see, and he makes me admit that my political career is a waste of time, while all that matters is just what I most neglect: my personal shortcomings, which cry out for the closest attention. So I refused to listen to him; I stop my ears and tear myself away from him, for, like the Sirens, he could make me stay by his side till I die" (216a–b).

There are few more powerful passages in all of literature about the power of our wills to refuse to listen to wisdom, to the truth. The very words of Alcibiades are mindful of that passage in Acts (7:57) that tells of the stoning of Stephen; at his famous speech, the members of the council "stopped their ears" so that they would not hear him, as if this deliberate non-hearing would excuse their actions. Such passages call our attention to the fact that, in a way, we can prevent ourselves from "really hearing" what we listen to or read. This is a rather frightening thought, even when we realize that we do hear the sound of what we refuse to comprehend and follow.

V

In Wendell Berry's novel *A Place on Earth*, there is a chapter with the wonderful title, "The Wanting of What May Be Lost." This is the other side of our refusing to listen to what is directed to us. We could probably not find a better description of our human condition than this title—all the most important things in our lives, in fact, may be lost. In one sense, if they could not be lost, they would not be worth having. Something of the whole notion of a free creation stands behind this idea. And yet such is our lot, that we can and do want what "may be lost."

In this chapter of Berry's book, the setting is Port William, a town in Kentucky along the Ohio River. Mat Feltner is the local farmer. His son, Virgil, has just been killed in action in World War II. Mat is with his son's wife, Hannah, who is pregnant with his grandchild. Mat reminisces on the character of his son as a young teenager who was learning how to farm. Virgil decided to plant a crop on a hillside, but he did not understand that the land was not prepared to protect the crop against soil erosion. It had too much of a slope. When a storm came, it wiped out the crop. The father knew Virgil was discouraged by his misjudgment of the land. However, Mat tells his son, "'Be sorry, but don't quit. What's asked of you now is to see what you've done, and learn better.' And I told him that a man's life is always dealing with permanence—that the most dangerous kind of irresponsibility is to think of your doings as temporary. What you do on earth, the earth makes permanent."[5] The soil eroded the land, but the permanent lesson remained, even with the death of the man it taught. Something Platonic exists in this passage. Plato was always searching for what is unchangeable admidst changing things. Even amidst things that are lost, permanent things remain.

Berry is a great lover of the land and so reminds us of its proper care. Like Plato, he is aware of the permanence of things, the forms that do not change, the cycles of the earth. But I particularly like that line, "a man's life is always dealing with permanence." This is especially significant when it is spoken while recalling his son, dead in battle. We have not here the "vanity of human wishes," but rather a sense of the permanence of things. "Celestial wisdom" calms the mind. Happiness may be something we do not yet see. Johnson's words recall the famous passage in the Epistle to the Hebrews: "Faith is the substance of things hoped for" (11:1). This too is part of wisdom.

VI

Just after the destruction of Mordor in *The Return of the King*, Sam Gamgee and Frodo Baggins are exhausted. They were isolated after their narrow escape, ashes falling all about, not knowing if they could leave the desolate area. Yet, realizing that they had succeeded in destroying the one ring, Sam knew he had been in an "experience," or an "adventure," to use the term Tolkien himself favored. Recall that at the very beginning of *The Hobbit*, we read: "This is the story of how a Baggins had an adventure, and found himself doing and saying things unexpected."⁶ The "doing" and "saying" things that are "unexpected" is precisely what indicates that wisdom is not totally under our control or simply a product of our own minds, even when it is indeed something we have acquired.

Looking back over the long adventure that he had joined and through which he persisted, Sam Gamgee reflected:

> "What a tale we have been in, Mr. Frodo, haven't we?" he said. "I wish I could hear it told! Do you think they'll say: *Now comes the story of Nine-fingered Frodo and the Ring of Doom?* And then everyone will hush, like we did, when in Rivendell they told us the tale of Beren One-hand and the Giant Jewel. I wish I could hear it! And I wonder how it will go on after our part."⁷

Sam Gamgee is perhaps the real hero of *The Lord of the Rings*. He is the ordinary man who can finally, after accomplishing his really heroic part, return home to Bag End, to Rosie, his family, and his land.

Frodo, as the ring bearer, is too broken, too wounded. Like Frodo, Sam is not one of the great ones of the universe. But this ordinariness did not prevent him from having a role to play that no one else could have performed. Without his contribution, the thing would not have worked, but he too, like Frodo, had to choose to accept his duty and be faithful to it. Sam's role was that of loyalty, while Frodo's was obedience. I recently came across a quotation from Dietrich Bonhoeffer, the German theologian, that said, "Only the devil has an answer for our moral difficulties, and he says: 'Keep on posing problems, and you will escape the necessity of obedience.'" *The Lord of the Rings* is about the necessity of obedience, as is, I think, the New Testament.

Yet, notice what it is that Sam wishes. He wishes to hear the tale of his exploits, of his experience, of his adventure as it is told again, almost as if to say that nothing is completed until we can hear it again. This would suggest that even though living through some love or adventure is the primary experience, it is never possible to exhaust what we are given in it without reflecting on it, putting it into place, seeing depths within it that we had missed the first time. The world does not only exist, but it exists to be known, and on being known, it further exists to be told about, to be recounted. This is why we can gain wisdom from tales, for the very hearing of them is a way of living. This is why we must read especially those tales and books that bring us, even vicariously, to *what is*.

Anton Myrer's war novel, *Once an Eagle*, records a scene after the end of the bloody fighting of World War I in France that, I think, explains something of this need of Sam Gamgee to hear his tale told. After months and months of constant fighting, the war finally ends. The hero, Sam Damon, is recuperating from a wound in a hospital in Cannes when, reflecting on what he has just been through, he realizes that "experience was valuable only if one imbued it with meaning, drew from it purposeful conclusions. The fact of the matter was he had never *thought*—he had acted, swiftly, intuitively; now he must school himself to think, think soberly and well."[8] This seeking to find thought in a completed action, to "think soberly and well," is much the same as Sam Gamgee's desire to hear about his own tale, and his wonder about how it would turn out after his time here had ended. Where things lead is also part of wisdom.

VII

Wisdom can come to us in many ways. Take, for instance, P. G. Wodehouse's amusing novel, *How Right You Are, Jeeves*. Jeeves is the very proper English valet to Mr. Bertie Wooster. Through his imposing Aunt Dahlia, Bertie has met a certain Roberta Wickham, whom his aunt is hoping may settle Bertie down in responsible marriage. Bertie suspects that this solution is fraught with dangers. As he tells Jeeves, the young lady, though quite handsome, is rather overly "enthusiastic." "The moment I cast an eye on her, it seemed to me that there was something strange about her aspect." She is out of sorts, in contrast to her normal self, which Bertie describes in the following manner in a phrase made famous by the philosophers. "Normally this beazel [beauty] presents to the world the appearance of one who is feeling that if it isn't the best of all possible worlds, it's quite good enough to be going on with till a better one comes along."[9] Our books of humor are often full of metaphysical insights, even theological ones, as we wonder what might be troubling someone in this good enough world.

The topic of the "best possible world" has long vexed the philosophers. Leibniz is said to have proved that this one we presently inhabit is indeed the "best possible one." For if the present condition is not the best possible world, what then is it? It boggles the mind. If, however, it is the best possible world, why is it so messy, even tragic? Roberta's solution, to see that it is "quite good enough to be going on with till a better one comes along," has much to be said for it. Wisdom does not deal primarily with what we wish we might have, but with what we do have. Even what we do not have or what we are not is part of our wisdom, in the telling of which, as Tolkien understood, we can also find a certain joy.

VIII

On the Monday before the Wimbledon Tennis Championship one year, Venus Williams made a comment that goes to the essence of sports: "The joy is to keep challenging yourself to keep on the top. If there was no challenge, there would be no joy." This comment brings us to the essence of wisdom, as sports often do. When Aristotle and Plato spent a good deal of time discussing sports, they were not being indifferent to what are considered the most important things.

"If there was no challenge, there would be no joy." This is a surely metaphysical sentence. If the best possible world is to exist, it seems that, at its heart, there should be a challenge of some sort, a world in which a failure or loss is at least possible. No challenge, no joy. This seems also to be the lesson of the adventure, of the experience of Frodo and Sam, even of Bertie Wooster.

Aristotle claimed, in a passage reminiscent of Plato's discussion of God's relation to the world, that games are played for their own sake. In this, Aristotle thought, they are like contemplation, in which we ultimately behold *what is* in itself. Aristotle understood how good games bring us outside of ourselves. Plato suspected that what we human beings—we "playthings of God," as he called us—really wish to do is to behold *what is*. What we really want is to both behold and respond to truth, to what is, not because we made it, but because it is given to us.

There is no joy without challenge.

There is no joy without actually seeking for, and possessing, the highest things—among which, in some degree, we already live.

As Wendell Berry said, "life is always dealing with permanence."

"*Aliis laetus, sapiens sibi.*"

"The proper operation of man as man is to understand."

"Every man is to take care of his own wisdom."

Chapter V

On the Consolations
of Illiteracy, Revisited

For of all my discoveries, nearly the most breathless was Dickens, himself. How many of the educated can ever suspect the delight of such a delayed encounter? I think we owned a *Collected Works* when I was a child. But I had tried *David Copperfield* too early and had believed all my life that he was not for me. One night last winter I was sleepless and somehow without a book. From our own shelves I took down *Little Dorrit*, which people tell me now is one of the least beguiling of the lot. But Keats first looking on Homer could have been no more dazzled than I first poring on my Boz. I felt as a treasure-hunter might feel had he tripped over the locked chest that belonged to Captain Kidd.

—Phyllis McGinley, "The
Consolation of Illiteracy"

Order in action is vital; order in action is impossible without order in thinking.

—Frank Sheed, "First Things"

Christmas time! That man must be a misanthrope indeed, in whose breast something like a jovial feeling is
not raised—in whose mind some pleasant associations
are not awakened by the reminder of Christmas. There
are people who will tell us that Christmas is not to them
what it used to be, that each succeeding Christmas has
found some cherished hope or happy prospect of the
year before, dimmed or passed away; that the present
only serves to remind them of reduced circumstances
and straitened incomes—of the feasts they once bestowed
on hollow friends, and of the cold looks that meet them
now, in adversity or misfortune. Never heed such dismal reminiscences.

—Charles Dickens, "A Christmas
Dinner"

I

Thus far, I have been speaking of learning, of books, even of "one's
own wisdom" in a most positive manner. Hence, it will, at first sight,
appear somewhat incongruous suddenly to suggest that there may be
any "consolation" for illiteracy. But the fact is that we can be literate
and still quite innocent of any real grasp of the meaning of things.
Likewise, we can observe that many of the most terrible movements in
the history of man have been led by men who, by any objective standard, were quite intelligent, even possessing the finest educations and
poetic talents. Again there are those who, for one reason or another,
were simply badly educated while in formal university or graduate studies. So, with some obvious paradox, it is not totally contradictory to
speak of the consolations of illiteracy. We may have been, unbeknownst
to us, saved from many a wrong turn simply because we did not know
such a turn was possible.

One of the most sobering passages in Plato is found in Book Seven
of *The Republic*, wherein he suggests that it is possible to learn or be
exposed to things too soon, or that it is impossible to learn many

things if we begin the project of learning them too early in life. This is definitely a countercultural, even shocking, view. To learn the highest things, it seems, we must first learn a multiplicity of things of lesser weight. In itself, this position does not deny that all things have their place and, as such, are good, even fascinating. The best things often take time, but we are loathe to admit it, let alone to wait till we are ready for them. The modern world opens too many flowers much too soon really to appreciate them in their full beauty.

Young potential philosophers are those who might eventually know the truth of things, but only if they would choose to undergo the discipline it takes to know anything *that is*. In a sense, one cannot be a philosopher without first being a potential philosopher. And no one can be a potential philosopher unless something moves him to wonder, unless he is struck by the being of something not himself. Even formed philosophers, as Plato said in the *Phaedrus*, can be struck by a reality outside of their system of ideas. Such an unexpected experience constantly reminds them that reality is greater than their philosophy, without denying, at the same time, that philosophy—the discipline that adds knowledge to *what is*—reveals the excitement in learning where we, both as individual persons and as human beings, stand in the order of things. We are intended both to know things and to recognize that we know them.

If they consider or experiment on something before they have either the maturity or judgment sufficient to examine it or recognize its evidence, young potential philosophers will easily become discouraged by the whole enterprise. They will think, because they did not easily see the point, that there is nothing there to be seen or learned, however highly it is praised by the dons, the sophisticated, the canon of great books, or the tradition. These disillusioned potential philosophers will suspect that the consideration of the things of the mind, of the things worthy to know for their own sakes, is a fraud and a deceit because they cannot effortlessly grasp them. But the highest things are, for our kind, conditioned on a period of advent and waiting. That we are not given all things at once is not a defect in our creation. It may well be part of its glory.

Plato, relying on natural reason and experience, did not think it possible for someone to be fully wise or mature much before he was fifty, and even then, only a few could become really accomplished. He also realized that we would die not so very long after fifty. Socrates, after all, was killed at seventy (Plato himself died at eighty-one).[1] If we were worthy, Socrates thought, on death we would pass to the Isles of the Blessed to carry on, still under the light of the good, the conversations begun in this life. While human nature might be the same in all times and places, human genius, effort, discipline, and virtue are not evenly distributed, nor would it be good if they were. To Socrates, the common good seemed to demand that those of the same nature should differ in many individual ways, even though all were created for the same ultimate destiny, the attainment of which was, in part at least, dependent on each person's own choices. A city composed of philosophers alone would soon fall into decay. A city in which no philosophers resided would lose contact with the very substance of what we are given to be.

At first sight, no doubt, we might think just the opposite—that the sooner we begin to learn about the highest things the better. Plato, of course, thought that we should begin whenever we are ready. The question is, when are we ready? Plato was content to let little children play their games, even though he was aware of the damage disordered games might cause in the souls of the young. There are things that we might do at twenty that we can or ought not do at ten or five, and things we might do at forty that we can or ought not at twenty. But for us to appreciate the highest things, we must learn early to rule ourselves, to rule our fears, our pleasures, our anger, even our wit. It is a gradual, even agonizing process, thought Plato. Neglecting this self-discipline, we will never be free to confront *what is*. Rather we will see everything in the light of our own inner disorders. The orders of polity, cosmos, and soul are interrelated. With disordered souls, we will not clearly recognize the truth of reality. We have to learn to rule ourselves, to master numbers and memorize words and poems. We need also to sing, ride, and dance. We should even play the flute, as Aristotle told us, but not too well, lest we neglect many other things.

Today, we sometimes seem to think that the great books can be learned in college, or in high school, or in grammar school, or even in preschool; after all, most of them are already online. I have seen a rather impressive great books program developed for homeschooling at the high school level, at which period in our lives we need to read much literature and poetry, play games, learn music, memorize, and, yes, speak. But there is a sense in which we may not be ready for the great books' deepest teachings at such a young age.

The whole of Book Seven of *The Republic* contains Plato's concise explication of the ages at which the educated man ought to learn each different kind of art or knowledge. This schema will, however, probably strike us today as having it all wrong. Our society seems to be filled with two kinds of educational innovation, the education of children at an early age, almost as if mothers and fathers did not exist—this too is a Platonic idea—and "continuing" education, which often means teaching those who did not learn much or enough at any earlier age, who did not, in short, learn how to learn. Indeed, it seems we even want to put "intelligence genes" in our babies before birth to supplement or replace what is given in nature. Whether, when subjected to such infusion, such offspring are still "our babies," or even more intelligent than they otherwise might have been, is seldom asked.

I realize that there is a kind of romantic attraction to the notion that we should always be "learning" from infancy to death. And there is no doubt that our lives can be pictured as a quest or journey. But we are not gods and, in the strict sense, we ought not want to be. We do not understand our ultimate divinization or grace itself to mean that "what it is to be a finite human being" will cease to exist. The human being is itself one of the orders of creation—a good. I have no problem, furthermore, in acknowledging the enormous amount of factual information available to us, the mass of which no one man can possibly know, nor needs to know. This vastness is why we have in existence precisely great numbers of our kind. Thus, the exigencies of our particularity do not prevent the actualization of other things to which we cannot ourselves attend, but through which we are made more complete.

II

Academic institutions are not ends in themselves, but way stations to something nobler. I like to ask the question, "What do we do when all else is done?" I do not conceive this to be merely a question about the transcendent vision of the good. Surely, the answer to this question is not that we always remain in school, even as professors, as if life consisted not only in high school diplomas, BAs, MAs, and PhDs, but in a never-ending accumulation of more and more credits and degrees. That is like preparing for preparation's sake, with no thought about what one is preparing for in the first place.

School is not an end in itself. The Greek word from which we get school, namely *skole*, means leisure. Leisure has the connotation of unendingness, of continued newness, of things undertaken for their own sakes. We can never fully fathom the mystery that any particular thing exists in the way it does. The famous "student prince," the carefree aristocrat who always desires to be young and romantic in the university, with its time apart from time, dwells in a perpetual "la-la land." He is an aberration. So are, as Plato also says, professors who imitate their students—or fathers who imitate their sons.

There comes a day, both sad and glorious, in which we "leave" school for good. We do not leave life, but we leave school. We cannot live a real life if we spend it thinking about, and recriminating ourselves for, what we do not yet know. Some things can only be known if we do not know them ahead of time. I suspect marriage is like this; children too. We need to leave space for gifts. This need to act on imperfect knowledge is what the virtue of prudence has traditionally been thought to be for. It is not a "fault" of our nature that we live in this evidently imperfect or incomplete world. Even though our minds are capable of knowing *all that is*, it is still all right that we do not know, say, all eight hundred languages spoken in the Congo or the complete works of Hegel in German. My paternal grandmother had a third-grade education. She was a very smart and wise lady. My father had a semester at college, just before the Depression. My brothers had BAs; I have a doctorate and a couple of MAs. Germany offers two different kinds of doctorates. One of my Austrian professors had five. Lawyers now also like to become doctors and vice versa. Yet what there is to know, what exists, has not changed from the time of creation, except in so far as ordered change has been an aspect of creation itself. Our capacity to know much about it, however, has changed, including the record of what we have learned about the world, God, and ourselves. Thus, there is both what there is to be known *and* what we know about what there is to be known—two steps, not just one.

Then too, I suppose, there are a lot of things that we have learned wrongly, granted that we cannot know error without also knowing at least something of the truth. The history of our errors is, as such, almost as interesting as the history of the truths we know. Indeed, as Aquinas implied, we do not really know truth unless we know what is opposed to it and why. This is, in fact, one of the dramatic ways in which thought differs from reality, at the same time that it is making reality itself known. It is a good thing to understand error and sin, and to accurately state what they are, for this too is a truth.

This inquiry is designed for those who do not doubt their capacity to know but who still have a "hankering" to know what they do not yet know. There are not a few today who think that education in general at every level is so bad or deformed that we are lucky if we are never even exposed to it in the first place. There is something to be said for realizing that we are often on our own if we want to seek and know the truth. At a conference in Wyoming, I once talked to a very intelligent and accomplished young woman who told me that she had been homeschooled all her life. I asked her if she had thought of going to college. She told me that she had considered it, but that she did not want college to interfere with her education. If she went to college and ran up a big debt to pay for it, she would have to have a job to pay it back. She would then never really be free to learn much of anything of true importance. The idea that college matriculation may be a kind of slavery that prevents us from being educated in the things that matter is startling, but the case can be made.

III

In the summer of 2003 I found myself in California with my brother and sister-in-law. One day, we decided to visit an older section of San Diego where my sister-in-law could check out the antique shops. It turned out that the shop where my brother and I were to meet her also had some used books. Looking idly through the shelves, I came across an old thirty-five-cent *Saturday Review Reader*. My sister-in-law bought this volume for me for a dollar, the difference in price over time itself being a lesson in economics: the value of thirty-five cents in 1954 would be significantly more than one dollar today. The essays in the volume were written between 1950 and 1954. Among them are Joseph Wood Krutch's "Is Our Common Man Too Common?" John Mason Brown's "The Trumans Leave the White House," A. Whitney Griswald's "Liberal Arts at Mid-Century," and Bennet Cerf's "Trade Winds."

The essay that struck me and provoked me to want to own the volume, however, was the one by Phyllis McGinley (1905–78), provocatively titled, "The Consolations of Illiteracy." It was a charming essay that began with these somewhat shocking words: "There is something to be said for a bad education." I certainly wanted to see what it was. McGinley was famous for her light verse, even for her poems on saints. One of her books was titled *Saint Watching*, and I recall her poem on St. Bridget. McGinley had pungent things to say about fathers, husbands, women, and just about everything else, including sin.

Of sin, she wrote, "sin has always been an ugly word, but it has been made so with a new sense over the past half-century. It has been made not only ugly but passé. People are no longer sinful; they are only immature, or underprivileged, or frightened, or, more particularly, sick." That is about as fine an analysis of the status of moral reasoning as I have seen in recent years. We were, in fact, more ourselves when sin was still an "ugly" word than we have become with its meaning being merely "sick." After all, if what we do is caused by immaturity, poverty, fear, or sickness, it is not, strictly speaking, sin. Sin includes will, and such words as "sick" or "immature" are usually employed to prevent us from seeing that sin cannot fully be explained by anything else *but* will.

This reflection brings to mind something I once read in Frank Sheed about St. Thomas Aquinas: "Ignorance of St. Thomas Aquinas varies from that of the Belfast judge who admired his *Imitation of Christ* to that of the educated Catholics who do not read him because they do not care how many angels can dance on the head of a pin."[2] We know, of course, that Thomas à Kempis, not Thomas Aquinas, wrote *The Imitation of Christ*, still one of the most widely read books in the history of the world. With regard to angels dancing on pins, Dorothy Sayers once wrote an essay titled "The Lost Tools of Learning," a truly magnificent essay, in which she pointed out that the medieval logical exercise about angels and pins was designed to make the point that angels did not have the category of "space." The point of the exercise had nothing to do with angels dancing but rather with the very nature of angels themselves as spiritual beings who do not occupy space. The medieval man would be amused by our misunderstanding of such basic points.

IV

Phyllis McGinley's essay is a remarkable and delightful sketch of what we can learn when we have, for one reason or another, thus far learned relatively nothing. I have often amusingly given the short form of the very long subtitle to my *Another Sort of Learning* as "how to get an education even if you are still in college." The danger of being in college, as E. F. Schumacher pointed out in *A Guide for the Perplexed*, is that a student may learn nothing of importance there, nothing that gets to the heart of things. Phyllis McGinley's essay, in which she speaks of "the splendors of discovery," might be called "how to get an education when you have been out of college ten or twenty years." Just because we may not "have learned" much, does not mean that we are doomed to learn nothing at all. Indeed, McGinley seems to hint that we may have some advantage if we have passed innocently through college and, for all we know, learned nothing in the process.

McGinley tells us that she went to a country school in Colorado, the proverbial one-room schoolhouse. On winter days, she and her brother were sometimes the only ones who showed up. "If there was a public library within practical distance, I never learned of it," she tells us. Her family was a "reading family," but there was not much to read at home—just her father's law and history books, and "the collected works of Bulwer-Lytton." Her high school was something of a disaster, where they were "always having to make reports on Ivanhoe" or memorize Burke's "Speech on Conciliation." She had to parse "Snowbound" twice.

Her college days were even worse. "My alma mater was one of those universities founded and supplied by the state, which in the West everybody attends as automatically as kindergarten. There are—or were then—no entrance examinations. Anybody could come and everybody did, for the proms and the football games; and they sat under a faculty which for relentless mediocrity must have outstripped any in the land." One cannot help but think, in retrospect, that such a school might well be preferable to those more recent ones with tough entrance exams and faculties corrupted in their souls by the latest ideologies. It is better to learn nothing than to have to unlearn much. Indeed, I suspect that McGinley's advice is as much designed for the latter group of students, victims of political correctness, as it is for the former, of which she was one. Her companions were ignorant, but they were not ignorant because what they were learning in college was untrue.

"Through a complicated system of juggling credits," McGinley tells us, "and wheedling heads of departments, I [was] able to evade even the Standard General Survey of English Literature." She did read some things, however. "I was even considered a bookworm by my sorority sisters, who had given up going to the library after polishing off *The Wizard of Oz.*" She read mostly contemporary books, "Mencken but not Marlowe, Atherton but not Austen." No Chaucer, no Dryden, no Herbert, no Donne, no Hopkins or Marvell. She lists some of the books and poems that she did *not* read—an infinite list even for the zealous, no doubt: *Vanity Fair,* "Il Penseroso," "The Hound of Heaven, " *Anna Karenina,* etc.

This sort of miseducation, she thought, had a certain hidden advantage. Students often do not read or want to read, such is the perversity of our nature, because they are *required* to read, because they are assigned to read. I do not know whether this reaction is one of the effects of the Fall, but it is often the case. "Almost none of the alleged classics, under whose burden the student is supposed to bow, had I peered into either for pleasure or for credit," McGinley confesses. But once she discovered such books, she read them excitedly because she wanted to, because she found them delightful. "Although I came to them late, I came to them without prejudice. We met on a basis completely friendly; and I do not think the well educated can always claim as much." Plato said that education should be a form of play or delight. McGinley discovered this truth for herself—in part because she had such a lousy education.

McGinley once felt sorry for people who *had* to read George Eliot's *Silas Marner* or *Adam Bede.* Then one evening, when she could find nothing else on her shelves, she actually read the latter book. She could only say to herself, "But it's magnificent." Eliot was not dull at all, as she had been told. She once pitied those poor souls who had to write papers on "Richardson as the Father of the English Novel." But then she read Richardson's *Pamela* as if it were "a brand new book." Indeed, this is how she read all books, new or old. Scholars, she says, may appreciate *The Deserted Village*, or *Pride and Prejudice*, or *The Old Curiosity Shop*, or *The Bostonians*. "I do not think, however, they feel the same proprietary delight as I do toward them. Behind those pages, for me, hovers no specter of the classroom and the loose-leaf notebook. Each is my own discovery." This is a very Chestertonian realization, the independent discovery of what already exists, and its abiding delight.

Thus does McGinley speak of her own discoveries—and, in the intellectual world, we can indeed "discover" what has been already discovered by someone else. Books are "possessed" because we read and re-read them, not because we own them, though ownership is a natural consequence of this delight in reading. All of us have shelves of unread books, and this is not all bad. Books become, on being read, our spiritual property, as it were. Once, still in college, McGinley discovered Mrs. Gaskell's *Cranford* in a "boarding house bookcase." As she read it, she kept telling her friends how charming it was, reading passages aloud to them. She then learned, much to her consternation, that nearly all of them had already read the book as an assignment as juniors, and that they had all "disliked it." In fact, she knew, they had never really read it. Their souls were not prepared for its delight. What a sad thing, to have souls not prepared for *what is.*

"There are books that one needs maturity to enjoy just as there are books an adult can come on too late to savor," reflects McGinley. She thinks *Wuthering Heights* needs to be read before sixteen, but "no child can possibly appreciate *Huckleberry Finn*." Then there is Jane Austen. "Had I been younger than thirty when I first happened on Miss Austen I might have found her dry. Had I read her much later I might have been too dry, myself." What a remarkable observation! In a sense, it is best to discover mature things when we are mature. This is why Plato tells us to learn numbers and arithmetic when we are young, and also to memorize the poets. He doubted whether we could be metaphysicians before we were fifty. Indeed, he thought that thinking about the higher things too soon would give us a distaste for them.

Moreover, there is a certain appropriateness in coming on things later in life. McGinley states, "I capitalize on my lack of impatience. I am not on fire to see everything at once." Though we are anxious to see the whole of things, if we understand our nature we will strive to be content to proceed step by step, gradually, as Aquinas recommended. "Because I am grown-up, I am under no compulsion from either the critics or the professors to like *anything*," writes McGinley. If we are under no "compulsion" to like anything, we can like what ought to be liked. We can trust our power of seeing and judging. We can be free to see what we might have otherwise missed were we compelled to see it.

McGinley, surprisingly, finds Trollope "dull." But that is nothing against Trollope, she admits. I myself stumbled on to *Barchester Towers* a couple of years ago. I found it the most delightful book I had read in years, a jewel. Its depiction of the non-celibate clerical life in the Anglican Church is more amusing and more sobering than any celibate cleric might otherwise suspect. Surely it should be required reading for all bishops of the Roman persuasion. Too, I was once in Australia where I found in some library a copy of Trollope's journals of his visit there in the nineteenth century. But I can accept that Miss McGinley finds him "dull." She knows that not everyone will.

McGinley's favorite is Dickens, a judgment with which I am sure Chesterton would agree. "For of all my discoveries, nearly the most breathless was Dickens, himself. How many of the educated can even suspect the delight of such a delayed encounter," she writes. She went through a stint of reading nothing but Dickens—*Great Expectations, Martin Chuzzzlewit, Oliver Twist, The Pickwick Papers,* and *David Copperfield.* After *Bleak House,* she stopped reading him, if only to catch her breath. "It's consoling to know the rest of the novels [of Dickens] are there waiting for me, none of them grown stale or too familiar for enjoyment." Chesterton, in his famous biography of Dickens, remarked that Dickens had created hundreds and hundreds of odd, amusing, and poignant little characters that no one could forget, almost as if he shared in the creative abundance of things.

In the end, McGinley confesses that "there is still much to deplore about my education." After reading her essay, we are hard pressed to know what it is. She knows that it is probably too late to read "Latin verse in the original or have a taste for the Brontës, and those are crippling lacks." This is why Plato insists that we ought to learn things in their proper order. He does not have much hope for remedial education, however conceived. And he has a point. If we begin with bad habits, we shall in all probability end with them. But Phyllis McGinley reminds us that there are exceptions.

Thus, the consolations of illiteracy are there to give us hope. Few start out well. We need not be defeated by a bad education, or by no education at all. Nor need we be defeated by our own bad habits, if we are willing to change them. Like Louis L'Amour, in *The Education of a Wandering Man*, we can still read each year and list what we have read and where we read it. "To have first read Dickens, Austen, and Mark Twain when I was capable of giving them the full court curtsy is beatitude enough for any reader. McGinley writes, *"Blessed are the illiterate, for they shall inherit the Word!"*

V

Let us, to conclude this chapter, take a second look at McGinley's final beatitude—*"Blessed are the illiterate, for they shall inherit the Word!"* The very fact that she capitalized "Word" recalls that the world itself was made *in the Word*, that the *Word became flesh* to dwell among us. I suspect McGinley intended us to recall this association of word and *Word*. What has she shown in her praise of illiteracy? She has not advocated that we remain unlearned, that we remain uninterested in books, that we remain illiterate. Rather, she has provided for us a way to read what we might not otherwise read if it had actually been "taught" to us in a formal setting, if we had been required, against our wills, to read it.

Our society often expresses horror at the fact of illiteracy, both local and worldwide. In this sense, of course, illiteracy refers specifically to those who cannot read at all. Yet, that very word also bears the connotation of a different form of ignorance, that of those who can read but do not, or even worse, of those who do not know what to read, or who read but who do not seek the truth of things. It is even possible to read so that we do not know, so that we can formulate theories to justify our not knowing *what is*.

The capacity to read is what frees us from time and space, without denying that we are creatures of time and space—a good thing in itself. Many things can be "discovered" that we already knew something about. The great consolation of illiteracy, on consideration, is the capacity to be surprised, to be charmed and delighted at what men have recounted to us about their lot and their lives. It is not sufficient to live our own lives. We are given minds in order that we might "live" many lives, in many times and places. Phyllis McGinley was right to remind us that we need not know everything. And this lack of constraint is what gives us the freedom to enjoy things when we are mature enough, curious enough to see them for the first time.

Does this mean that nothing much can be learned while we are young, or are in college? Does this mean that we can learn nothing if we are "required" to learn it? These questions touch on the vexed question of what it is to be a teacher. Christ was simply called a "teacher," though He denied it. Socrates was said to be a teacher; he denied it, too. Phyllis McGinley probably should not be understood as opposed to learning anything in school in order that we might have the delightful experience of learning it outside of school. But she is certainly right in depicting the experience of reading. She is also right to go around buttonholing friends to listen to what she has just found in some book they never heard of, or may have read but never were moved by.

It has always struck me that both reading aloud and reading silently to ourselves are active/passive experiences. That is, through reading we encounter what we did not previously know. To do this, we must be open to what we do not already possess in our souls. Monks still have the custom of "reading at table." That is, for a main meal, someone will read from a book, usually not too heavy, but still of some note, profundity, and delight. Margaret Craven, the author of *I Heard the Owl Call My Name*, tells us that she moved away from San Francisco to Palo Alto so that she could devote herself to writing. "For the first time I realized that professional creative writing is the only craft that must be practiced in silence and solitude."[3]

Likewise, any reading, light or heavy, requires "silence and solitude." And, to recall a famous remark of Cicero, we are not really alone when we are alone in this way. Reading is a contemplative act. It is a beholding of what we do not already possess. And one of the things that strikes us most about reading is that when we encounter something that strikes us as true or even as funny we long to share it with someone. We sense that a thing is not complete until we have spoken it to someone else, anyone else. This is, in part, what Aristotle meant when he said that we are social and political animals.

"Order in action is impossible without order in thinking," Frank Sheed told us after the manner of the great tradition. Even if we come at reading haphazardly, we should not forget that what we are doing is seeking order for our souls. One of the consolations of "illiteracy" is the possibility of our finding this order even when we do not find it in our formal education. Surely this is essentially what Phyllis McGinley meant.

Let us not forget these propositions:

1. "For all my discoveries, nearly the most breathless was Dickens, himself."

2. "Order in action is vital; order in action is impossible without order in thinking."

3. When someone tells us Christmas has been diminished, "Never heed such dismal reminiscences."

4. *"Blessed are the illiterate, for they shall inherit the Word!"*

Chapter VI

ON KNOWING NOTHING
OF INTELLECTUAL DELIGHTS

The Classical Struggle between Poetry and Philosophy

Since bodily pleasures are vehement, they are sought by those who cannot enjoy other pleasures, i.e., by those who, since they know nothing of intellectual delights, incline only to physical pleasures.

—Thomas Aquinas, *Commentary on Aristotle's* Ethics

But in case we are charged with a certain harshness and lack of sophistication, let's also tell poetry that there's an ancient quarrel between it and philosophy. None the less, if the poetry that aims at pleasure and imitation has any argument to bring forward that proves it ought to have a place in a well-governed city, we at least would be glad to admit it, for we are aware of the charm it exercises.

—Plato, *The Republic*

In this world, we must be prepared for anybody to say anything.

—P. G. Wodehouse, *Pearls, Girls, and Monte Bodkin*

The Life of the Mind

I

We can acknowledge, with Phyllis McGinley, that there is something to be said for avoiding a bad education if it leaves us free to find our way to a good one. In this chapter, however, I want to take such reflections a step farther. I will suggest that there is, in fact, a danger in not having a genuine intellectual life. I do not mean that we must all be an Aristotle or an Aquinas, but I do suggest that we are not complete as human beings if we do not have a real taste for learning and take a real delight in it. I do not intend this chapter to be a polemic against pleasures, but an argument for them. It is an effort to relate pleasures to the order of things in which they originally exist. If we neglect the higher pleasures, we will consequently be prone to mislocate other pleasures. Hence, we will not really be prepared to appreciate them.

On Saturday, April 5, 1760, Samuel Johnson wrote in *The Idler* that "the only end of writing is to enable the readers better to enjoy life." Let us not forget, then, that Scripture is the written Word of God. And let us suppose, also, that writing can be successful, that it may achieve its purpose. Need we inquire whether enjoyment itself requires further justification? Could there be life with no enjoyment? What indeed is the relation between life and its enjoyment? We have heard of "the Man of Sorrows." He is the same man who said to a thief, "This day thou shalt be with me in paradise" (Luke 23:43). Paradise is not a place of sorrows.

Aristotle spends a good deal of time on the subject of pleasure, in part because he realizes that it is one of the main factors that encourages us to do or know what is worthy. It can likewise *prevent* us from seeing or understanding what it is worthwhile to do or know. Indeed, it is, paradoxically, a pleasure both to talk about pleasure and to understand it in all its varieties. It is worthy of investigation for its own sake, just so that we know what it is. Besides the relish of actually beholding them, understanding that *things are* and *what things are* is itself a delight. Indeed, aside from the experience of pleasure itself, a distinct intellectual pleasure is found in understanding the essence of any kind of pleasure, including physical pleasure. Our minds always reflect back on our experiences.

Aristotle even suggests in Book I of *The Ethics* that pleasure, along with money, honor, and contemplation, can serve as a possible "definition" of human happiness. Indeed, we have probably met people who do define their happiness in this manner. All that they propose to themselves to do or make is considered in the sole light of their pleasure-seeking. Aristotle does not think pleasure per se to be an adequate definition of the happiness we seek and to which we are ordained in our very being. But he understands perfectly well how people come to think that pleasure might be their purpose. Thus, he soberly warns us at the end of Book II of his *Ethics* that "we have more of a natural tendency to pleasure, we drift more easily towards intemperance than towards orderliness" (1109a14–16). Yet, some pleasure seems to be intrinsic to all that we do. The goodness or badness of a pleasure, moreover, always relates not to itself, to the pleasure, but to the goodness or badness of the act in which it is found.

Aristotle, moreover, does not oppose "pleasure" to thought or spirit. Rather he says that there is a pleasure intrinsic to everything that is worthwhile to do or think or make. To be pleased at what is worth being pleased about is the essence of our being human. As a sign of this truth, Aristotle points to some things that we would still want to do even if they did not, at the same time, also bring us pleasure—"seeing, remembering, knowing, having the virtues," for instance (1174a4–6). This profound insight reveals the distinction between pleasure and the action in which it normally exists. It does not deny that, though pleasure and the action in which it exists are always together in one and the same experience, they can be intellectually distinguished. We can attend to the one over or against the other.

We often think that pleasures are to be conceived in relation to their opposite pains. But, in a careful reflection, Aristotle reminds us that the "pleasures of mathematics, and among pleasures in perception, those through the sense of smell, and many sounds, sights, memories, and expectations as well, all arise without previous pain" (1173a16–19). That things delight us is far from being something to worry about, as if it were somehow sinful to take delight in what is delightful. (We should be worried if they didn't delight us, worried that the world is not properly made—a real worry for many who think there is no order in the universe, to be sure.) Just the opposite is true: we are made to delight in things—in smells, in sights, in mathematics, in our memories, and in our expectations. Being is not narrow or parsimonious, as we are too frequently tempted to believe.

"Every faculty of perception, and every sort of thought and study, has its pleasure," Aristotle explained, "the pleasantest acting is the most complete, and the most complete is the activity of the subject in good condition in relation to the most excellent object of the faculty. Pleasure completes the activity" (1174b21–24). We are not the cause of the being that can be delighted—that is, of ourselves—even when we are in fact delighted with something that is not ourselves. One of the great mysteries of the world, indeed, is the astonishment that things do delight us, give us pleasure. We are dull of mind and heart if we have never been struck by the fact that things actually exist that can give us delight; that some relationship exists between us and the world, a relationship that, apparently, neither we nor the world caused.

Contrary to common opinion, joy is more difficult to explain than suffering. Pleasures are more difficult to account for than pain. Pain at least has a purpose—to point to the location of the hurt. But pleasure exists for its own sake, even when the act in which it exists relates to something else. Notice that Aristotle said a person in his best condition experiences the most delight when he is confronting, or thinking, the highest object of his highest faculty, his intellect. When speaking precisely of our highest faculty and its highest object, Aquinas puts forth his notion of the Beatific Vision as the only object that can fully cause us to "rest," to use Augustine's phrase. Indeed, Aristotle himself hints at the same idea: "For activity belongs not only to change but also to unchangingness, and indeed there is pleasure in rest more than in change" (1154b22–23). The very idea of an activity in "rest" leads us to the most profound of considerations, not the least of which is the glimpse it provides into the nature of Trinitarian life.

II

In large part, culture consists in the ability to relate the pleasure of a thing to the object of the action or thought in which the pleasure properly exists—the right time, the right place, the right circumstances. In *Pro Archia*, his speech on the liberal arts, Cicero reminds his auditors of the power of poetry to honor the city and those noble deeds and virtues for which it stands. Evidently, Cicero tells us, Alexander the Great used to have with his armies a great number of historians who were supposed to record his famous deeds—a form of vanity, no doubt, but then the deeds of Alexander really were great and we are glad that they were recorded.

"And yet," Cicero tells us, "as he [Alexander] stood beside the tomb of Achilles at Sigeum, he uttered these words: 'Fortunate youth, who found Homer to proclaim your valour!'" Cicero goes on to explain why Alexander was right to have such a sentiment. For "if the *Iliad* had never existed, the tomb where Achilles' body was buried would have buried his memory as well" (ix, 22). Indeed, we are less concerned with our bodies than with our memories. In this sense, poets are more important than generals and politicians. The polity with no one to sing its praises, that is, with no poets, will soon disappear among men, unknown and unlamented.

Alas, the poets are not usually emperors, except perhaps in the case of Marcus Aurelius and his *Meditations*. Marcus Aurelius urged us to "let [our] delight and refreshment be to pass from one service to the community to another, with God ever in mind" (VI, 7). This, at least, is what one emperor wanted us to remember. But Marcus's life was marked by sadness, not enjoyment. We sometimes wonder why. Was it because he did not know the world was created in enjoyment and abundance, not necessity and determination? Can one's philosophy cause sadness? The great Stoic ideal was to achieve "apathy," or a studied indifference to pleasure and pain, in other words, to a rejection of all that Aristotle stood for. Indeed, what is peculiar to Stoicism, a philosophy by no means dead, is, as Charles N. R. McCoy used to say, a heightened sense of pride—a refusal to accept the world and hence one's mortal being.[1]

Think, however, of the pleasure of music. Plato devotes a good deal of attention to music, both as a philosophical and as a political phenomenon. He remarks, almost as an aside, that a change in music (and in sport) indicates a change in polity. Furthermore, Aristotle suggests that, as part of our education, we should all learn to play the flute, but only to play it badly—a passage reminiscent of Chesterton's great remark that if a thing is worth doing, it is worth doing badly.

In any case, we should know enough about music, Aristotle thought, to be able to understand and follow it. But we should not spend all our time practicing and perfecting an instrument as if we were professional artists who had little room for anything else in our lives. Aristotle warns that the lover of the flute is so distracted when he chances to hear it played, that he hears nothing else but its music. The flute was a wild, untamed instrument for the Greeks.

Plato, it is said, asked that the flute be played by a young Thracian maiden on the evening he died. When she hit a wrong note, he indicated the proper tune with his finger. This was his last act in this world, an act worthy of Plato, since it indicated the harmony of the world even in death. Still, Plato was quite certain that, while music could move us to our depths, it could also, almost without our noticing it, corrupt our very souls and cities by attuning them to patterns of emotional disorder. We underestimate the power of music and its rhythms at our peril.

Our souls and our bodies are joined together as one being and thus make one person, not two. We are not spirits imprisoned in a body, but incarnate souls. Everything about us, as Leon Kass pointed out in his wonderful book, *The Hungry Soul: Eating and the Perfection of Our Nature*, is reflected in our bodies, whereas what is without touches our souls through our senses. In this sense, our whole body is our instrument. We are bound to the world in everything we do and see and hear, and it, in turn, is bound to speak to us what it is. Yet in this very seeing and being bound, we transcend the world; we wonder why and how all that is fits together, even if what is not obviously ours is given to us. Reality seems to relate *being* to *gift*, almost as if that were its origin.

Chesterton, I believe, remarked that, as children and adolescents, we should memorize and recite poetry for the delight of its sound and rhythm, even if we did not yet understand it. That way, when we are old enough to understand it we will have the double pleasure of knowing the words by heart—something more easily accomplished when we are young and our memories sharp.

I have often been envious of friends and teachers who have memorized long passages from Shakespeare, Dante, Scripture, Horace, or even "The Shooting of Dan McGrew." They can, when the occasion calls for it, recite these passages with vigor and depth, even with humor and song. The same is true of the capacity to play the piano, or to sing an aria, or to play the bagpipe. In reading Belloc, for example, as we shall discuss in more detail in the next chapter, how often do the music and the singing of long memorized tunes, often with their raucous words, come into his books, especially his walking books, such as *The Path to Rome* and *The Four Men*.

As P. G. Wodehouse's Monte Bodkin says, "We must be prepared for anybody to say anything," including, I suppose, what the heretics say, what is false as well as what is true. Notice that Wodehouse says that we must be "prepared" for this eventuality, as if somehow we might not expect that "anything" could happen. That is to say, in spite of his exclusion from the city of those poets who enticingly portrayed the gods and heroes doing corrupt things, Plato still invited back the poets of order. He understood the power of charm and rhythm.

Anybody can speak the truth. Anyone can deny it. As Aristotle said, we are to listen carefully both to truth and to what is not true. "We must, however, not only state the true view, but also explain the false view, since an explanation of that promotes confidence. For when we have an apparently reasonable explanation of why a false view appears true, that makes us more confident of the true view" (1154a23–26). To repeat young Bodkin's trenchant words, "We must be prepared for anybody to say anything." But we also must be prepared to understand why anybody says anything, including what is false.

We can and do, no doubt, overemphasize the function of pleasure in our lives. Yet in a way, today we almost seem more likely to underestimate it, particularly the pleasures of the highest things. "Neither intelligence nor any state [habit]," Aristotle remarked, "is impeded by the pleasure arising from it, but only by alien pleasure. For the pleasures arising from study and learning will make us study and learn all the more" (1153a22–23). Thus, Aristotle actually states that from "study," that is, from theory or contemplation, a positive pleasure arises that we need to experience. If we do not experience this pleasure, we really have no idea of that to which we are directed in our being as the "rational animal," the being who knows what is not merely himself—who knows himself, in fact, only as a function of knowing something that is not himself. Aristotle adds, frankly, "pleasures [do] impede intelligent thinking, and impede it more the more we enjoy them; no one, e.g., while having sexual intercourse, can think about anything" (1152b16–18). This observation is not intended either to denigrate intercourse or thought, but to recall their proper nature and relationship to the whole of what human life is about.

Clearly, Aristotle does not deny that there are different kinds of pleasure, some of which rightly impede our thought. But, as St. Thomas Aquinas, in his calm way, said in his commentary on this passage, it is sometimes rational to be irrational. Neither Aristotle nor Aquinas would deny the reality of pleasure. Both recognize its diversity and relation to the realities that give rise to it. Indeed, in a famous passage,

Aristotle displays his monumental common sense in this regard: "Some maintain that we are happy when we are broken on the wheel, or fall into terrible misfortunes, provided that we are good. Willingly or unwillingly, these people are talking nonsense" (1153b19–20). Aristotle was not a Stoic. Aristotle is surely the philosopher most acutely aware of what is happening when, as he says, we are "talking nonsense."

III

When we presume to speak of a "struggle" between poetry and philosophy, we are, of course, immediately confronted with the immense mind of Plato, who brought this famous struggle to our attention in the tenth book of *The Republic* (607b). To understand this contest we must first consider the great questions: "What is poetry?" "What is the city?" "What is philosophy?" As Leo Strauss once remarked, not the "how does it work?" question, but the "what is?" questions are the most important ones, particularly the question, "*Quid sit Deus?*"[2] This last question, "What is God?" is the last sentence in Strauss's book *The City and Man*, his examination of classical political philosophy. Strauss is the modern thinker who most carefully draws to our attention that the first word of Plato's *Laws* and the last word of *The Apology* is *theos*, the Greek word for God. What is to be noted about this question, "*Quid sit Deus?*" is that Aquinas in the *Summa* only inquires about "what God is" *after* he had first answered the question, "*An sit Deus?*"— "does God exist?"

The ancient stories of the gods are cast in the form of "myths," stories that explain to human cities their origins and the order of their polity. It is of these things that the poets sing: the founding of cities, the defense of cities, or, in the case of Virgil, the refounding of cities. Socrates was accused of atheism, that is, of not believing in these gods of the city, even though he stoutly maintained that he did believe in spirit and therefore, logically, in spiritual beings. He contrasted the gods of the poets with the god of the philosophers. He was scandalized by the activities of the gods depicted in Homer, so he wanted to banish the poets who praised such gods from his city in speech. He wanted there to be at least one city in which the right order of the soul was recognized and maintained even if its existence was only in speech. All education begins with reading *The Republic,* so that in every historic polity with all its inevitable imperfections we will be able to keep alive in our souls the reality of the best city, the highest object, as Strauss says, of the study of political philosophy as such.

Recall the famous discussion of time in *The Confessions* of St. Augustine. "What, then, is time?" writes Augustine. "As long as no one asks me, I know. As soon as I wish to explain it to him who asks, I know not" (XI, 14). On Wednesday, April 10, 1776, in a dispute about the poetry then in fashion, Boswell, in some exasperation, asked Johnson, "Then, Sir, what is poetry?" Johnson replied, "Why, Sir, it is much easier to say what it is not. We all know what light is; but it is not easy to *tell* what it is."[3] We all recognize what poetry is, what philosophy is, but we are hard pressed to explain or define either with any exactness.

"All things by nature have something divine in them," Aristotle remarked in a profound passage (1153b32). This statement recalls Aquinas's thesis about the preservation in being of *what is,* that it cannot stand outside of nothingness by itself. A contingent being does not cause itself to exist and existence can only be caused by existence, or what is. Thus, if it is outside of nothingness, if it exists, it cannot do so by itself, but needs what causes existence. If there really is "something divine" in all things, then the statement that all things are "interesting" hardly indicates the profundity of any thing we encounter. And to know what all things are, to know the whole, is what philosophy is about, or at least what it seeks to know. The essential difference between philosophy and poetry is that the latter seeks to know all things through one thing; whereas the former seeks to know the place in being of all things insofar as they are related to each other, including the highest things.

What is distinct about Christian revelation in its relation to philosophy is that it proposes that all things are made intelligible by that center wherein the divine meets the human, that is, in the Incarnation, in the Person of Christ, in the Word made flesh. It proposes that all things, in themselves, are unnecessary—that, quite contrary to determinist theories, they are rooted in unnecessity. They need not be, but are. If they are, they must have their source in the Divinity that goes out from Himself in a free way. In this sense, all things exist first after the manner of gift, of the love that causes the world to be and orients it back to its source through the divine plan in which it exists, through the Word.

In his brief comment on the dedication of the John Paul II Cultural Center in Washington (*L'Osservatore Romano*, November 13, 2002), Pope John Paul II remarked, "The mission of the center is inspired by the firm conviction that Jesus Christ, the Incarnate Word of God, is the center of human history and the key which unlocks the mystery of man and reveals his sublime calling." There exists a "mystery" about man. He has a "calling." His "calling"—that to which he is ordered or "pulled," to use Eric Voegelin's terminology—is precisely "sublime." Human history has a "center." At this center is the Incarnation, the Incarnate Word. This is where man is explained to himself. And we do want to have ourselves "explained," as it were. Our intellects seek faith, seek to know the full meaning of *what is*, without denying that they do not know everything by themselves.

IV

In an old *Peanuts* cartoon, we see Schroeder, with great concentration, playing an obviously complicated piece of classical music, the notes of which are pictured coming out of his piano. Lucy lies on her back against the piano faced away from him. Her eyes are closed in meditation. In the second scene, Schroeder looks directly at her as she puts her elbows on the piano. She affirms, cheerily, "That's beautiful, Schroeder, what is it?" In the next scene, while Lucy still looks on admiringly, Schroeder is back at the keyboard. He answers firmly, "The First Prelude and Fugue from the 'Well-Tempered Clavichord' by Bach." In the final scene, Schroeder has a frown on his face as Lucy rolls back over, looking away from the piano. "It's beautiful anyway," she concludes matter-of-factly.[4]

Much of what I am trying to explain in this chapter is contained in this charming scene from *Peanuts*. Lucy is not an artistic sophisticate like Schroeder, but she is extremely clever. She does not care for the names of pieces and composers. She does not know Bach from Tennessee Ernie Ford. But she does not let much get by her. She has a crush on Schroeder, who does not give her the time of day, partly because she is so dumb about or perhaps indifferent to music, especially the compositions of his hero Beethoven. But here she shows a new side. She cannot help but recognize that this piece is beautiful. She admits it. She even asks "what is it?"—the *"what is?"* question. Schroeder tells her its name, but this sort of factual knowledge is no help. She knows, in the end, that "it's beautiful anyway." Something has touched her.

In his book *Heart of the World, Center of the Church*, David Schindler wrote that "giving glory to God is a comprehensive task for Christians, occupying not only all of their time but also all of their faculties, their mind as well as their will."[5] When Lucy hears a piece of music, she knows it is beautiful. She wants to know *what it is*. She is, in her own way, involved in giving glory to God by saying of what she hears that it is beautiful. This affirmation would be as true if she said it of a sunset. And we cannot freely and consciously "give glory" unless we first are the kind of beings who have the power or capacity to give glory—unless we are the kind of beings out of whom glory-giving can arise.

The title of this chapter is "On Knowing Nothing of Intellectual Delights." This phrase comes from Aristotle. He remarked that if we knew nothing of intellectual delights we could not be captivated simply by knowing *what is*. This lack of appreciation for intellectual delights is particularly characteristic, Aristotle thought, of politicians, though I suspect it also characterizes many academics and clerics. Lacking the pleasure of intellectual delight, we tend to seek a kind of pleasure that knows nothing of the intrinsic purpose of knowledge. Our minds do seek to know. What is perhaps unique about Christianity is that it is a revelation that unabashedly also addresses itself to intellect. It recognizes that everyone, philosopher or not, needs to be properly directed to the highest things, to that to which we are ordered in the very structure of our being. We also need first to be receivers, to be open to what is not ourselves so that we are able to respond to *what is*.

Let me cite one last passage from Aristotle: "For in the case of human beings what seems to count as living together is this sharing of conversation and thought, not sharing the same pasture, as in the case of grazing animals" (1170b12–13). In the Last Supper, John recalls to us the remarkable conversation in which Christ said to His disciples that He would no longer call them servants but friends. Looked at objectively, this is probably the single most important passage in our literature, since it shows that philosophy and revelation belong to the same discourse, the same reality. It gives a divine answer to a profoundly human question. And Christ gives a reason for calling his disciples friends. They are not merely animals who graze in contentment. Rather, they can exchange thought about the highest things. In fact, He tells them that they are His friends because He has "made known to them everything that He has learned from the Father" (John 15:15). He has made known to them the Trintarian inner life of God and their relation to it. If this be true, we are naturally drawn, in response, to give glory, to acknowledge the beauty of *what is*, not because we made it or comprehend it, but because we delight in knowing it even as we do not know it fully.

Thus, one of the functions of revelation is not merely to explain to us what things Christ has learned from the Father, but to instruct us in how properly to give glory, since not every way is suitable to the God *who is*. This is why the words "I no longer call you servants but friends" are to be understood in the light of "Do this in memory of Me." And this latter command must itself be understood in the light of the Word made flesh who dwelt among us and who, while so dwelling, was crucified under Pontius Pilate, died, was buried, and rose again on the third day. This is the "myth" that is true—the story, as Chesterton said, that is "too good to be true." It is also, as Tolkien wrote, an *eu-catastrophe*, a happy catastrophe. It is one of the things that the mind must think about when it considers ultimate things.

In the ancient struggle between philosophy and poetry, Plato only allowed that poetry back into his city which was beautiful in what it held about the gods, in its rhythms, and in its melody. He knew that in the end there is only one way to counteract music or philosophy that does not glorify God as He is supposed to be glorified, and that is to produce a counter-poetry, a counter-music that is even more beautiful. To grasp the central point of Christianity in the intellectual sense means, whether we agree with it or not, to acknowledge that this poetry or myth has been produced, and that its production is not wholly something of human origin, that we did not ourselves produce it.

The poet who outshone Homer, whom Plato loved, was none other than Plato himself. The very reading of Plato is a step toward the right ordering of our souls, even our Christian souls. When we, as Christians, read and are moved by the poetic charm of Plato we can at the same time know that we have also been given a specific revelation, an account that is addressed to our very minds and through them and our bodies to the cosmos. We are aware that Christianity includes the Cross, hardly a beautiful thing. And yet, we hold that Christ is the Word in whom all things were made. We are to re-address all things in this light, even sufferings, even the Passion of Christ, as Bach himself did in his glorious music of *The Passion According to St. Matthew*.

When it comes right down to it, this Passion remains among us in the sacrifice of the Mass. "The one event on Calvary that we commemorate and reenact," Robert Sokolowski has written, "was first anticipated, before it occurred, by Jesus. It was anticipated and accepted by him as the will of the Father."[6] With Plato himself, mankind has long searched for the proper way to address the divinity. We should not be surprised if men could not find such a way by themselves. We know that there is real pleasure in knowing the highest things. And in the end, we are even more delighted to know that our questions and searchings were so worthy that they have, in fact, been responded to. We have only to listen—and yes, on listening, to sing and to dance. It is for this reason that we are called to glory, and to give glory. *Gloria in Altissimis Deo* (Luke 2:14).

Chapter VII

THE METAPHYSICS OF WALKING

There, the great Alps, seen thus, link one in some way to one's immortality. Nor is it possible to convey, or even to suggest, those few fifty miles, and those few thousand feet; there is something more. Let me put it thus: that from the height of Weissenstein I saw, as it were, my religion. I mean, humility, the fear of death, the terror of height and of distance, the glory of God, the infinite potentiality of reception whence springs that divine thirst of the soul; my aspiration also toward completion, and my confidence in the dual destiny. For I know that we laughers have a gross cousinship with the most high, and it is this contrast and perpetual quarrel which feeds a spring of merriment in the soul of a sane man.
——Hilaire Belloc, *The Path to Rome*

The Greek word *philosophia* is a path along which we are travelling. Yet we have only a vague knowledge of this path.
——Martin Heidegger, *What Is Philosophy?*

There is not upon earth so good a thing as an inn, but even among good things there must be hierarchy. The angels, they say, go by steps, and I am very ready to believe it. It is true about inns. It is not for a wandering man to put them in their order, but in my youth the best inn of the inns of the world was an inn forgotten in the trees of Bamber.

—Hilaire Belloc, *The Four Men*

I

At first sight, this chapter will seem out of place. "Intellectual delights" seem to be a far cry from walking. Nonetheless, this chapter is about walking and, as such, it is also about the life of the mind. It is a chapter about the walks of Hilaire Belloc, the English man of letters, who has written more on walking than almost anyone. What does this consideration about walking have to do with reading, with the "intellectual life," with learning? In a way, everything. And why do I associate metaphysics, perhaps the most difficult of intellectual disciplines, with walking? It is not merely a paradox, I think. There is a difference between walking a mile on a country road and knowing that the exact distance we traversed is one mile. The former experience brings us to the *things that are* in a way that mathematical distance, though not to be neglected, cannot.

Books are not first intended to take us to other books, though there is nothing wrong if they do. We have seen that Aquinas takes us to Aristotle and Augustine takes us to Plato. Books are intended to take us to *what is*. Books are intended to guide us to see both what is visible and what is invisible. We sometimes think that the highest things are learned apart from the ordinary things. But it is not true. The greatest philosophers, in a sense, affirm what we already know, what we already see. So, as in all of the chapters of this book, we have here another way of seeing. We discover a way of looking about while we walk, and a way of walking that takes us to the knowledge of *what is*—to metaphysics, the science of being as being, as they say.

If we be Platonists or Aristotelians, as I hope we are, we must, in some sense, also be peripatetics, that is, those who learn by walking about, usually about our cities if we be Greeks, about our countryside if we be English. Socrates is said to have left Athens only once, aside from the army, and that was for the walk in the countryside described for us in the *Phaedrus*. Socrates asks Phaedrus where he has been and where he is going. Phaedrus replies, "I was with Lysias, the son of Cephalus, Socrates, and I am going for a walk outside the city walls because I was with him for a long time, sitting there the whole morning. You see, I'm keeping in mind the advice of our mutual friend Acumenus, who says it's more refreshing to walk along country roads than city streets" (227a). Socrates had no trouble, at least on that particular day, agreeing with this preference for walking in the countryside on a hot day.

We should recall that Cephalus, the father of Lysias, was the elderly gentleman in the beginning of *The Republic* who was upset that Socrates did not come down to the Piraeus (seaport of Athens) to see him, since Cephalus himself was old and could not easily get around the city anymore. Socrates, however, protests that he in fact enjoys talking to old men, for they are able to teach him how it is best to traverse a path that we all must follow (328c–e). This passage reminds us that the very symbol of walking is itself an analogy for the path of our lives from conception to death and beyond. We have come from somewhere and we have someplace to go—as Chesterton said at the end of *Dickens*, the road ultimately leads to the inn, not the inn to the road. Or, as Socrates put it, "We might ask those who have travelled a road that we too will probably have to follow, and what kind of road it is, whether rough or difficult or smooth and easy." Though Cephalus was rich, he still worried about his life, how he had lived it, what he must do to repair his errors. He obviously understood that the road led to a place to which he must eventually go.

I was born and raised in small-town Iowa, where walking in the countryside was part of my youth. I have lived much of my later life in three cities—Rome, San Francisco, and Washington—each of which is simply a walking city, a city of seeing and hearing. Each city must be seen on foot to be seen at all—even of Los Angeles, the city of automobiles, I can only say that, in spite of its vastness, it is full of places in which it is pleasant to walk. Such cities do not allow us simply to "see" them. To see such cities, we must wander about them again and again over a long period of years. How did each city come to be? Why are we there, seeing it?—these are our questions. Walking is not mere exercise, and we can, with a little effort, take walks on most of our fleeting days.

II

I do not visit a place, a city, a countryside, in which I do not try to walk, even if only for a brief while. I was once, for instance, in Stamford, Connecticut, a place about which I knew exactly nothing at the time. I had forty-five minutes to walk its downtown streets. The noises, the spaces, the smells, the movements of people, of animals, of machines, all are important. Nothing assures us that a place is real more than walking it, its roads or sidewalks or even its grass. When we put our foot down, the ground on which to step is already there. We did not put it there, nor give ourselves the two feet with which we walk. Once we recognize that something is in fact "real," that it *is*, we can begin that second adventure of our existence, which is not only to know that something besides ourselves exists, but to inquire about what it means. *Omne ens est verum*. Without knowing, existence is not complete. For this latter project, as a sure guide, no one is better than Hilaire Belloc.

"The love of a village, of a manor, is one thing," Belloc wrote in an essay titled "On Old Towns." "You may stand in some place where you were born or brought up, especially if it be some place in which you passed those years in which the soul is formed to the body, between, say, seven years of age and seventeen, and you may look at the landscape of it from its height, but you will not be able to determine how much in your strong affection is of man and how much of God."[1]

Indeed, how much of our affection is of man and how much of God?—this is an ultimate question.

Just before her seventy-seventh birthday, my step-sister, Mary Jo, now in Clarksville, Tennessee, told me that she and her son hoped that summer to visit the town in Iowa in which we had gone to school, just so that her son, now a grown man, could see the houses and places in which his mother had once lived. This wondering about the physical dimensions of our origins is close to Belloc's point. Even in ourselves, we cannot easily distinguish among those things that are most important to us, which ones come from man and which ones from God. In the project of knowing ourselves, it is not sufficient to know that we are born of our parents, though we do know this immediate origin and want to know it.

This consideration, likewise, brings to mind the *Crito* of Plato, particularly the famous conversation of the Laws of Athens with Socrates. The personified laws remind him that his parents' bond of marriage was according to Athenian custom. In other words, our very origins have something about them that is already out of our control: the first meeting, accidental or divine, of our parents. This is particularly true if we believe that the soul which informs our particular body is immortal, directly created by the divine power alone. It does not cause itself. Though we look like our parents, or our grandparents, the light in our eyes is from eternity.

Thus, in encountering even ourselves, we encounter more than ourselves. We know that our response to the Delphic command, "Know Thyself," is at best inadequate. We find out rather soon that in knowing ourselves, we must know first what is not ourselves. We are not the direct object of our own knowledge. We know ourselves indirectly in knowing something other than ourselves. We are set free to know, in fact, by almost anything that is not ourselves. In this sense, all physical things transcend themselves in our knowing.

But a walk in England, or France, or Africa, or Spain, or California, each a memorable site of a Belloc walk, is not, at first sight, nearly so solemn as our very births. Can we really speak of the "metaphysics" of walking? Metaphysics, after all, is a rather heavy word. We can so speak only, I think, if walking puts us singularly in contact with reality, with *what is*, with what is not ourselves. Rousseau, in the second of his *Reveries of the Solitary Walker*, writes:

> Having, then, formed the project of describing the habitual state of my soul in the strangest position in which a mortal could ever find himself, I saw no simpler and surer way to carry out the enterprise than to keep a faithful record of my solitary walks and of the reveries which fill them when I leave my head entirely free and let my ideas follow their bent without resistance or constraint. These hours of solitude and meditation are the only ones in the day during which I am fully myself and for myself.[2]

But Belloc, who sometimes seems like a singularly lonely man, is closer to the truth. He is fully himself when the subject of his musings is not himself. Rousseau, on the other hand, almost seems to think that his freedom consists in removing real things from his reveries so that he can think without being grounded in or encumbered by an order of things not of his own making. Belloc's solitary walks are very different, as we shall see.

III

A "metaphysics of walking"? Are we alone when we are alone? Cicero said that he was never less idle than when he was by himself. Belloc, himself once a student at John Henry Newman's Oratory School in Birmingham, began his essay on the city of Arles in France in a way that only could be done by a Christian reader of the Greek classics—that is, by one who could combine metaphysics and history, the knowledge of things and the things themselves.

The use and the pleasure of travel are closely mingled because the use of it is fulfillment, and in fulfilling oneself a great pleasure is enjoyed. Every man bears within him not only his own direct experience, but all of the past of his blood: the things that his own race has done are part of himself, and in him is also what his race will do when he is dead. . . . History, therefore, once a man has begun to know it, becomes a necessary food for the mind. . . . But history if it is to become just and true and not to become a set of airy scenes, fantastically coloured by our later time, must be continually corrected and moderated by the seeing and handling of *things*.³

Metaphysics is the science of being *qua* being, of first things and their causes. We are astonished that something, including ourselves, stands outside of nothingness. Even to meditate on nothing, we must begin with something not ourselves. Belloc probably would not have called himself precisely a professional metaphysician (if indeed there is such a thing). Yet, I was pleased to come across by chance, on the Internet of all places, the preface that Belloc wrote in 1927 to Vincent McNabb's book, *The Catholic Church and Philosophy*. I have touched on this essay in the introduction to this book. Belloc used the word "discovery" in connection with philosophy. He understood that he must make clear how this word, "discovery," applied to philosophy— itself an adventure in the discovery of *what is*. To "discover" something implies that it is already there. That is, we do not, contrary to much modern thought, concoct the content of what we think about out of our own minds. Unless something already exists, we cannot "encounter" it.

"Philosophy signifies primarily the love of knowledge—ultimate knowledge upon the ultimate realities," Belloc wrote,

and, by extension, it especially signifies the solving of questions which the mind puts to itself relative to the most important subjects with which the mind can deal. Thus this word "discovery" is especially applicable to the philosophic function—the action of the mind when it succeeds in philosophical research. For instance, one of the prime questions man asks himself is whether his personality be mortal or not. The answer given to such a question is the supposed solution of a problem, and if the answer is true it is a discovery. Or again, a process of reasoning which establishes the existence of a personal God is a discovery.[4]

Plato speaks of an *eros* that compels us to seek to know the highest things. Notice that Belloc's emphasis is not merely on philosophy as a "questioning," which would make it merely a kind of misguided Platonism, but rather as an answering, which bears hints of Aquinas. The real discovery is not that we have questions, but that we have answers to such questions. Our minds cannot be satisfied with mere questioning, even though to question is to start to seek an answer.

IV

Needless to say, when one deals with Belloc and walking, one thinks both of the inns at which Belloc rested—recall the inn at Bamber—and that this inveterate walker was also a sailor—*The Cruise of the Nona* is Belloc's book about sailing around the British Isles. In the passage on Arles, as we have seen, Belloc never loses sight of the metaphysical need to "see and handle" actual *things*. He constantly reminds us that *things are*, that we cannot find out about them unless we look at them, feel them. Belloc also reminded us that we are attached to the past and future of this very race of men to which we belong. In Belloc, the land symbolizes the reality that we know and need to examine. The sea is our call to something beyond ourselves.

"I never sail the sea but I wonder what makes a people take to it and then leave it again," Belloc wrote in an essay titled "On Sailing the Seas."

To sail the sea is an occupation at once repulsive and attractive. It is repulsive because it is dangerous, horribly uncomfortable, cramped and unnatural; for man is a land animal. . . . A man having sailed the sea and the habit having bitten into him, he will always return to it: why, he cannot tell you. It is what modern people call a "lure" or a "call." He has got it in him and it will not let him rest.[5]

Belloc understood that within us there is indeed a "call," even a "restlessness" that draws us out of ourselves. In spite of his concreteness, there is something almost Platonic about Belloc. He does not minimize the difficulties of sailing ships. He knows man is "a land animal."

Later in the same essay, Belloc is speaking of his "own small harbours of the Channel," places full of men who go to sea. Then he talks of the Morbihan, the land and coast of South Brittany and the peninsula of Quiberon. The men there "produced vast ships rigged with iron chains, and boasting leathern sails, yet having nowhere, you would think, whither they could trade." What were they about?

The Romans under Julius Caesar, Belloc tells us, once defeated these men of Morbihan in the waters "north of St. Nazaire." "But what a fight they put up! I think they must have gone to sea for the mere love of it, these men of the Morbihan, as do their descendants to this day. For they are all poor men and get little from their occupation beyond dreams and death."[6] The practical Caesar executed the defeated sailors of Morbihan lest there be further naval threat from that direction. But I ask you, is there a finer sentence in the English language than this one of Belloc's?—"For they are all poor men and get little from their occupation beyond dreams and death."

V

The last essay in Belloc's *Hills and the Sea* is titled "The Harbour in the North." It begins, "Upon that shore of Europe which looks out towards no further shore, I came once by accident upon a certain man."[7] As far as I can determine this unnamed harbor is on the northeast side of Scotland looking north to the Orkneys and the Arctic Ocean. Belloc had sailed into this little harbor and dropped anchor in low tide. In the silence of the morning, he heard a man "crooning" to himself. He spotted him in a nearby boat. The boat was "sturdy and high, and I should think of straight draught. She was of great beam. She carried one sail and that was brown," Belloc carefully tells us.[8]

Belloc struck up a conversation with the man, who answered "in a low and happy voice." He said, "I am off to find what is beyond the sea." Belloc naturally wanted more particulars: "to what shore?" he asked. The man replied, "I am out upon this sea northward to where they say there is no further shore." The man seemed to have a plan. He had prepared for a long voyage and had something almost mystical about him. When Belloc pressed him further, the man replied:

"This is the Harbour in the North of which a Breton priest once told me that I should reach it, and when I had moored in it and laid my stores on board in order, I should set sail before morning and reach at last a complete repose." Then he went on with eagerness though still talking low: "The voyage which I was born to make in the end and to which my desire has driven me is towards a place in which everything we have known is forgotten, except those things which, as we know them, reminded us of an original joy."[9]

The man said that there was also a harbor in the South. He did not know the happy people there, but thought they would receive him. When he reached his destination, he said, "I shall come off the sea for ever, and every one will call me by my name." The sun was just rising and Belloc did not get a good look at the man, but he thought by his voice he was from "the West."

Realizing that what this man sought was something transcendent, Belloc told him, "You cannot make this harbour; it is not of this world."[10] At that point, the wind rose and the man sailed out of the Harbor in the North, keeping a steady tiller until he was out of Belloc's sight. Belloc then concludes both the essay and the book in the following exalted manner:

> Oh! My companions, both you to whom I dedicate this book and you who have accompanied me over other hills and across other waters or before the guns in Burgundy, or you others who were with me when I seemed alone—that ulterior shore was the place we were seeking in every cruise and march and the place we thought at last to see. We, too, had in mind that Town of which this man spoke to me in the Scottish harbour before he sailed out northward to find what he could find.

And so Belloc tells us of the lure present in every adventure on land or sea. We seek an ultimate harbor or home in all we seek, a place where we are reminded of "an original joy."

The poets and the philosophers, at their best, also tell us of such things. But in the end, as Belloc tells us quite soberly, "I did not follow him, for even if I had followed him I should not have found the Town." As Augustine said, the City of God, the "Town" of God, is not of this world, but that does not mean, contrary to Machiavelli, that it does not exist.

VI

Treves (Trier) is the oldest city in Germany, dating back to the time of Constantine. It is one German town that Belloc rather liked, mainly because it bears in its very foundation something older and larger than Germany itself. "All that great transition from the pagan to medieval Europe one feels more at Treves even than one does at Aix; and this, I suppose, is because the roots of Treves go deeper; but partly, also, because Treves is more of a border town."[11] Gothic had penetrated to Treves within a century after its arrival in Paris. Belloc went into the Church of Our Lady in Treves, and there he found "something even more astonishing than its early witness to the Western spirit of Treves."[12] To the "left of the choir," he found a small freestone statue of Our Lady "of the most heavenly sort." No one had much photographed this statue; no one seemed to know much about it. But it was far better than the vulgar things he had seen in Metz, Berlin, Posen, and Liepsic.

Then Belloc gives us another insight into the metaphysics of walking, into the necessity of actually seeing and touching things, of allowing things actually to crash into our world:

> Seeing such a noble statue there, I thought to myself of what advantage it would be if the people who write about Europe would really travel. If only they would stop going from one large cosmopolitan hotel to another, and giving us cuttings from newspapers as the expressions of the popular soul! If only they would peer around and walk and see things with their own eyes![13]

We are to "peer around," "to walk," and finally "to see things with our own eyes." But we live in a time when our epistemology often does not allow us to trust our own eyes. We see but we do not believe that what we see has its own existence.

VII

The person most responsible for our not seeing what is there to be seen is, no doubt, Descartes. In Belloc's *Characters of the Reformation*, he devotes one chapter to Descartes (1596–1650) and one to Pascal (1623–62), both of whom he considers to be representative of the philosophy that formed modernity:

> In the midst of these political figures, Kings and Statesmen and Soldiers, whom we have been considering in connection with the great religious struggle of the seventeenth century, we must run for a moment to two men who had no political power. They were neither Soldiers nor Statesmen nor men of any hereditary position; but they influenced the mind of Europe so greatly that their indirect effect weighs more than the direct effect of others.[14]

Belloc saw the origins of "rationalism" in Descartes and of "emotionalism" in Pascal, while also noting that both men remained orthodox all their lives, a sobering thought about the relation of faith and knowledge.

Belloc considered Descartes a great mind. From him we have "the tendency in all philosophy called 'modern' which till lately grew more and more skeptical of mystery, less and less concerned with the unseen, and more and more occupied with matters susceptible of repeated experiment and physical appreciation."[15] This is rationalism, which holds that what we know is not really the thing examined, but rather what our method allows us to know, and to know on our terms.

As Belloc put it, "We mean by the Cartesian rationalism that habit of subjecting all examination of reality (that is, all search after truth) to a certain process which is called 'that of the reason' and 'the reason only.'"[16] Both Descartes and Pascal were "great mathematicians," that is to say, men who studied extended matter without motion. In the thought of both, the things of the spirit became detached from the examination of being.

Descartes systematically eliminated from knowledge everything he could doubt until he finally arrived at what apparently he could not doubt: his own existence. But even that certainty was based on the postulate that what he knew besides himself required, not a knowledge of real things, but a proof for the existence of a God who would not deceive us. Belloc thought Descartes' postulate "I think, therefore I am" to be true, but he also pointed out that it was the "postulate of a sceptic, and has acted ever since as a poison."[17] That "poison" prevents us from knowing the real relation of ourselves to what is not ourselves.

We are not only aware of our own existence. This is not the only thing we cannot doubt. Belloc, in a profound passage, puts it this way:

> For there is another thing of which we are also just as certain, really, as we are of our own existence—and that is the existence of things outside ourselves. There is no rational process by which the reality of the external universe can be discovered; all we know is that it can be confidently affirmed. Aristotle, who might be called reason itself; St. Thomas Aquinas, whose whole process was that of beginning with a doubt, and examining all that there was to be said for that doubt before the denial of it and the corresponding certitude could be arrived at, both postulate this second truth. Not only am I, I, but that which is not myself is just as real as I am, and what is more, can be and is apprehended by myself.[18]

The "whole stream of modern skepticism" flows from Descartes. Belloc perceptively notes that one of the problems with modern European philosophy occurs when scientific evidence itself begins to suggest that the separation of "matter and spirit" is not as absolute as Descartes thought it to be.

VIII

This brings Belloc to Pascal. "Pascal began like a man moved suddenly by a vision or a great love."[19] Pascal made his reputation in dispute with the Jesuits of his time, who "had made it their business to reconquer Europe for the Church." There is an individualism present in Pascal's thought, which bears an element of truth. "In a sense the individual is everything; it is the individual soul that is damned or saved and the Church is only there to help a man to save it." But in emphasizing this majesty one can be led to belittle the divinity.

The Jesuits were thought by Pascal (and later by Nietzsche) to be too lax. Most people, Belloc thought, could make the proper distinctions between the law and exceptions to the law—they could see the difference between murder and self-defense, for instance. But he saw that the emotionalism of Pascal had an ironic future. "It is worth noting, by the way, that the most sentimental people, who are loudest against the right to wage a just war, or execute a criminal, are just the people who are most likely to be in favour of 'putting incurables out of their pain,' which the commandment against murder most emphatically forbids."[20]

Belloc thought that Pascal's understanding of the simultaneous greatness and misery of man was his greatest insight. But he saw in Pascal's emotionalism the roots of a morality that ended up denying any objective order. "In Emotionalism the action of the conscience is not that of a deductive rational process, or even that of an experiment or of an appreciation of an object from without. It is an internal imperative order, which does not base itself upon a thought-out process or a deliberately sought experience, but on the immediate sense; it is an emotion, and nothing but an emotion, of right and wrong."[21] Belloc comments on the irony that both men remained in the faith, even though their respective systems led either to skepticism or "to a contempt for doctrine and a sort of cloud over the mind in which men lose the Faith."[22]

IX

Belloc's boat once sailed into the port of Lynn, on the River Ouse, in Norfolk, off the Wash into the North Sea. "Every man that lands in Lynn feels all through him the antiquity and the call of the town," Belloc observed.[23] Once ashore, Belloc was struck by the specifics of the place, its resistance to centralization. There is something very English, or at least ancient English, about Belloc. "It is not only that the separate things in such towns are delightful, nor only that one comes upon them suddenly, but also that these separate things are so many. They have characters as men have. There is nothing of the repetition which must accompany the love of order and the presence of strong laws."[24] That there are so many particular things is itself a cause of wonder.

Belloc had been in Lynn some nine years before his present visit. He wondered if the Burgundy wine at the Globe tavern was as good as he remembered. Lynn was once called "Bishop's Lynn," but Henry VIII renamed it "King's Lynn." Belloc, however, still sees the Gothic presence there going back to the bishop's times in the borough. "There is everywhere a feast for what ever in the mind is curious, searching, and reverent, and over the town, as over all the failing ports of our silting eastern seaboard, hangs the air of a great past time, the influence of the Baltic and the Lowlands." Even in failing, silting towns, we can find feasts for the eye if our mind is curious, searching, "for these ancient places do not change, they permit themselves to stand apart and to repose and—by paying that pricealmost alone of all things in England, they preserve some historic continuity, and satisfy the memories of one's blood." There is a romanticism in Belloc that allows him, wherever he might be, to be refreshed by the being of what he finds. "So having come round to the Ouse again, and to the edge of the fens at Lynn, I went off at random whither next it pleased me to go."[25] All things are created good, and we should strive to know them.

X

Let me conclude this chapter with a series of aphorisms and statements drawn from this chapter on the "metaphysics of walking." Cumulatively, I think, they will serve to remind us of what we have encountered in these reflections.

1. "For I know that we laughers have a gross cousinship with the most high."
2. "There is not upon this earth so good a thing as an inn."
3. "But you will not be able to determine how much of an affection is yours and how much is of God."
4. "History must be constantly corrected and moderated by the seeing and handling of things."
5. "Philosophy signifies the solving of questions which the mind puts to itself relative to the most important subject with which the mind can deal."
6. "For they are all poor men and get little from their occupation beyond dreams and death."
7. "The voyage which I am born to make is towards a place in which everything we have known is forgotten, except those things, which, as we know them, remind us of an original joy."
8. "Oh! My companions . . . that ulterior shore was the place we were seeking in every cruise and march and the place we thought at last to see."
9. "If only they would peer around and walk and see things with their own eyes."
10. "Not only am I, I, but that which is not myself is just as real as I am."
11. "I went off at random whither next it pleased me to go."

Seeing, handling, sailing, thinking, touching, dining, traveling, and, yes, walking—such are the paths that lead us to metaphysics, to *what is.*

Chapter VIII

BEYOND DESCRIPTION:
ON "THE MOST WONDERFUL BOOK"

> At seven in the morning we reached Hannibal, Missouri,
> where my boyhood was spent. I had a glimpse of it fifteen
> years ago, and another glimpse six years earlier, but both
> were so brief that they hardly counted. The only notion
> of the town that remained in my mind was the memory
> of it as I had known it when I first quitted it twenty-nine
> years ago. That picture of it was still clear and vivid to me
> as a photograph. I stepped ashore (from the fast boat of
> the St. Louis and St. Paul Packet Company) with the feel-
> ing of one who returns out of a dead-and-gone genera-
> tion. I saw the new houses—saw them plainly enough—
> but they did not affect the older picture in my mind, for
> through their solid bricks and mortar I saw the vanished
> houses, which had formerly stood there, with perfect dis-
> tinction.
>
> —Samuel L. Clemens, *Life on the
> Mississippi*

I

Let me return from walking to reading, to another book, though the
setting of these remarks in this chapter has to do with Napa, California. Belloc's wife Elodie was in fact from Napa, and he travelled across

the United States twice to woo her. Napa is a place I have rarely had the pleasure of visiting. There is a small high school there, Trinity School, where I was once asked to give the commencement address, an occasion that always draws our attention to the potential philosophers, to the lives of minds just beginning to be aware of what there is to be known. What does one tell young students in such a setting as Napa Valley? It is, I think, the same thing I have been saying throughout these pages: there are wonderful things to be read. Life is, to be sure, more than reading, but it is still not complete without our being ready to lose ourselves in a book that delights us.

If someone has the privilege of attending grammar school and high school in Napa Valley, he probably knows more about grapes and wine than anyone else of his own age, except perhaps those who live in the Bordeaux or Chianti regions. Yves Simon remarked somewhere that the child of a doctor is likely to know something more about biology or anatomy than is the child of a Buick or Toyota dealer, while the latter will probably know more about the workings of automobiles than simply how to turn on the ignition. In other words, it is perfectly all right to learn something from our family or from the place in which we live. Some perverse philosophers would destroy the family because of such natural advantages. In fact, many if not most of the things one most needs to know about life may be found within one's own household, or at least within the city limits.

We should not, then, be entirely surprised that someone, even our parents, learned something before we came along. One of the burdens of being young is that it usually takes, as Plato calculates it in the seventh book of *The Republic*, until one is about fifty years old to figure out most of the essential things one needs to know. Not a day passes in which we did not learn something we might have learned. There is nothing necessarily tragic about this, unless we think we are gods. Yet, we would be a little inhuman were it not unsettling to realize that we might easily have learned something but did not take the opportunity to do so.

Aristotle has something even more fundamental to say about the need for a proper upbringing. We need to be brought up in "fine habits, if we are to be adequate students of what is fine and just, and of political questions generally," he tells us.

> For the origin we begin from is the belief that something is true, and if this is apparent enough to us, we will not, at this stage, need the reason why it is true in addition; and if we have this good upbringing, we have the origins to begin from, or can easily acquire them. Someone who neither has them nor can acquire them should listen to Hesiod: "He who understands everything himself is best of all; he is noble also who listens to one who has spoken well; but he who neither understands it himself nor takes to heart what he hears from another is a useless man." (1095b4–12)

We do not want to be useless men. We do not want to be among those who have not understood the simple fact that "something is true," a fact that we should learn first at home. Someone who cannot figure out such a truth or learn it from another simply cannot understand what his life is about.

Aristotle suggests that we do not need to know everything from the beginning. But we do need to accept the premise that "something is true," from which affirmation all valid things flow. Something *is* true. Much of modern thought and much of modern academic life are built on a denial of this assertion. There usually follows from this denial an effort to abolish the very idea of truth in the minds of students who learned it, as Aristotle says, from their upbringing.

It was George Bernard Shaw, I believe, who once quipped that "youth is wasted on the young." But if we do not waste any time at all in our lives, especially when we are young, we probably have never really been youths. The Little Prince, in a book everyone ought to have read, affirms that it is only the time that we "waste" with our friends that matters. Getting to know one another is not a question of science; it has a lot to do with just being together with nothing "to do." If we are always busy, always preparing for something else, we will never be able to attend to the important things—to which someone besides Plato should tell us to attend. On second thought, perhaps Plato is sufficient to tell us these things. Much of what is called education is the realization that Plato has already told us most of what we need to know.

II

On October 25, 1944, J. R. R. Tolkien wrote a letter to his son Christopher. In it, Tolkien cited a letter that he had himself received from a young man by the name of John Barrow, who at the time was twelve years old and attending "Westtown School, Westtown, PA." Tolkien was then in the process of writing his famous *Lord of the Rings* trilogy.

This is the letter: "Dear Mr. Tolkien, I have just finished reading your book, *The Hobbit*, for the 11th time and I want to tell you what I think of it. I think it is the most wonderful book I have ever read. It is beyond description. Gee Whiz, I'm surprised that it's not more popular. If you have written any other books, would you please send me their names."[1] In a footnote, Tolkien remarks that he was quite surprised to learn that American boys really used the expression "Gee Whiz!" (I rather doubt that it is still much used today.) We need not add that, in retrospect, young Mr. Barrow need not have worried about the popularity of Tolkien, whose tales became the most widely read books in the twentieth century and probably so far in the twenty-first century.

Over the years, I have had students in my classes at Georgetown who have told me that they have read the whole of Tolkien's trilogy every year since they were ten or eleven years old. They would agree with the young man from Westtown, PA, that this book—if I may assume that *The Hobbit* and the trilogy are really just one book—is "the most wonderful" there is. It is no mean thing, I think, to encounter such a book when one is under twelve, even if one does not fully understand what it is all about. The book's very charm is enough to alert us to its fundamental significance. I do not think that I read Tolkien until I was in my sixties. I even reread his books in lieu of seeing the movie versions, which I fear will in a way deprive me of the actual texts.

One of my former students advised me against *The Lord of the Rings* movies. He did not think they retained the sense of joy that suffuses and underlies the books. I suspect he is right. Something powerful happened to the boy in Westtown because he read Tolkien's book. "What exactly is it that happened to him?" we might ask. "Can it happen to us?" How do we find something that is "beyond description," and yet still try to describe it? For it is one of the abiding themes in this book that a thing is not complete until it is understood and some attempt is made to describe it, however inadequate.

One of the most famous books from antiquity is Plutarch's *Parallel Lives of the Noble Greeks and Romans*. This book is the source of several of Shakespeare's plays and indeed has been treasured by all generations since it was written in the early part of the second century A.D. (45–120). Probably no book gives us more graphic examples of how we ought or ought not to live than does Plutarch's. In his "Life of Cato the Younger" (95–45 B.C.), for instance, we read that

> Cato's natural stubbornness and slowness to be persuaded may also have made it more difficult to him to be taught. For to learn is to submit to have something done to one; and persuasion comes soonest to those who have least strength to resist it. Hence young men are sooner persuaded than those that are more in years. In fine, where there is least previous doubt and difficulty, the new impression is more easily accepted. Yet Cato, they say, was very obedient to his preceptor, and would do whatever he was commanded; but he would also ask the reason, and inquire the cause of everything. And, indeed, his teacher was a very well-bred man, more ready to instruct than to beat his scholars. His name was Sarpedon.[2]

Though few will likely bear the first name "Sarpedon," we certainly do presume and hope that our instructors will be "well-bred" and "more ready to instruct than to beat" young scholars! And as scholars ourselves, we must be ready to "inquire the cause of everything." We shall see shortly that the young Socrates manifested this very quality.

III

Linus and a very cute little girl by the name of Lydia are seen walking back from the ice cream shop. Lydia is in front of Linus and over her shoulder politely tells him, "Thank you for the Chocolate Sundae, Linus." This intriguing response naturally encourages a smitten Linus, who responds perkily, "You're welcome. Maybe we can do it again sometime." But Lydia suddenly turns on poor Linus, now completely deflated, to tell him, "I don't think so. I don't find you very interesting."

In the next scene, a forlorn Linus is seen in the yard sitting against a tree, understandably depressed that the charming Lydia finds him dull. But soon we see Lydia comfortably seated in a big couch in her home. She is on the telephone. We hear her say, "Hi, Linus. This is Lydia." Linus, still crushed, replies, "If you don't find me very interesting, why did you call me?" Lydia explains "There's nothing on TV."[3] Given a choice of nothing or Linus, even Lydia chooses Linus. This is what I will call "the Lydia academic principle." When it comes to things that really count, there is nothing on TV. Almost anything, even poor Linus, is better than the nothing that is on TV. Thus, my advice is always first to go to one of those wonderful books which are so often beyond description, however much we might occasionally learn or mislearn something from TV. Always seek to "find the cause of everything" before finding that there is nothing on TV. Nothing, strictly speaking, will teach one precisely nothing.

IV

In Psalm 119, we read, "I have no love for half-hearted men: my love is for your law" (113–14). I have long been struck by that phrase, "half-hearted men." Allan Bloom, in his *Closing of the American Mind*, spoke of college students with "flat souls." That is likewise a devastating phrase. Half-hearted men with flat souls—what could be worse? Would it be worse to believe that what is false is true? Plato said that truth is to know "of *what is* that it is, and of what is not, that it is not." Error is to affirm of *what is* that it is not. Thus, at first sight, we seem to be worse off if we have a head full of errors than if we are half-hearted or have flat souls.

Yet it seems, in a paradoxical way, that it might well be worse not to care about knowing anything important than to have a mind full of lively errors that we think are true. One of the seven cardinal sins is sloth, which is not the same as laziness. Rather, the slothful never try to understand who they are, never ask themselves any objective question about their purpose in reality. To be slothful is to consistently avoid ever having to live according to what we ought to be, based on who and what we are and our intrinsic purpose. In this sense, it is quite possible to be enthusiastic about many things and still be half-hearted men when it comes to the higher things. Indeed, pleasure and business, even education, have long served as a kind of escapism, a strategy proven to help us avoid examining our lives.

In his last day in jail, Socrates spends his time discussing with those around him the reasons why he does not escape or show signs of unsettlement about his dire condition. At one point he talks to Cebes about his own youth. "When I was young," he tells Cebes, "I had an extreme passion for that branch of learning which is called natural science; I thought it would be marvelous to know the causes for which each thing comes and ceases and continues to be" (97a). But Socrates admits that he never really could solve these sorts of questions. The ordinary answers given for them, referring to earth, air, fire, and water, did not satisfy him. Finally, however, in the midst of his perplexity he "once heard someone reading from a book (as he said) of Anaxagoras, and asserting that it is Mind that produces order and is the cause of everything" (96e). This explanation, Socrates says, "pleased me." We have here no flat soul, no half-hearted man, but one who was passionately interested in finding the truth of things he could not understand.

V

Henry Adams entered Harvard College in 1854. He was the grandson of John Quincy Adams, the sixth president of the United States, and the great-grandson of John Adams, the second president of the United States. The family on both sides had gone to Harvard before him. Among the other hundred students or so in Adams's class at Harvard was the son of a colonel in the Second United States Calvary by the name of Robert E. Lee. The nickname of Lee's son was "Roony." Though at first Adams thought the handsome young Lee was a leader, by the end of his four years at Harvard, he changed his mind. "He was simple beyond analysis; so simple that even the simple New England student could not realize him. No one knew enough to know how ignorant he was; how childlike, how helpless before the relative complexity of school."[4]

But Adams was even harder on Harvard. "Four years of Harvard College, if successful, resulted in an autobiographical blank," he remarked, "a mind on which only a water-mark had been stamped. The stamp . . . was a good one. The chief wonder of education is that it does not ruin everybody concerned in it, teachers and taught." After departing Harvard, Adams sometimes debated whether in fact it had not ruined him and most of his companions. Still, "Harvard College was probably less hurtful than any other university then in existence. It taught little, and that little ill, but it left the mind open, free from bias, ignorant of facts, but docile."[5]

Surely we do not want our education to ruin us. We prefer to be taught "little" than to be taught falsehoods, which is what Phyllis McGinley meant by the "consolations of illiteracy." Not that our minds should not be so open or free of bias that we stand for nothing and recognize no distinction in things. We do want to be "docile."

In Latin, the nominative form of this adjective "docile" is *docilitas*. It means the virtue of being able to be taught. The very name of this striking virtue implies that we must at some point choose to be taught. Only the proud cannot and will not be taught. Pride means, quite literally, that we are closed to everything but ourselves. If we are proud we allow ourselves to learn nothing because we think we already know everything, or perhaps that only what we know is worth knowing. This is the worst of human conditions. If sloth is the cardinal sin that refuses to examine our purpose in this world, pride is that cardinal sin at the heart of all other sin and disorder of the soul. It wants not to discover what is worth knowing, but positively to decide whether anything is worth knowing at all.

Samuel L. Clemens tells of reaching his old hometown of Hannibal, Missouri, on the packet boat of the St. Louis and St. Paul Lines, at seven in the morning. It was a Sunday. He walked through the town, feeling like "a boy again." In his memory, all things were again fresh. Clemens encountered an old gentleman who had been in Hannibal for twenty-eight years, arriving the year after Clemens had left. Clemens told the old man his name was Smith and inquired about his old school friends. Of the first one, the old gentleman replied, "He graduated with honor in an Eastern college, wandered off into the world somewhere, succeeded at nothing, passed out of knowledge and memory years ago, and is supposed to have gone to the dogs."

Of the brightest lad in the village, the man recalled, "He, too, was graduated with honors, from an Eastern college; but life whipped him in every battle, straight along, and he died in one of the Territories, years ago, a defeated man." Cautiously, Clemens inquired of the girls, especially of his early sweetheart. "She is all right," the man reflected, "been married three times, buried two husbands, divorced from the third, and I hear she is getting ready to marry an old fellow in Colorado somewhere. She's got children scattered around here and there, most everywhere."

This was not too promising a beginning. Another friend had been killed in the Civil War. Finally, Clemens mentioned another boy whose fate, it turned out, reflected one of the most curious enigmas of our nature. "There wasn't a human being in this town but knew that that boy was a perfect chucklehead; perfect dummy; just a stupid ass, as you may say. Everybody knew it, and everybody said it. Well, if that very boy isn't the first lawyer in the State of Missouri today, I'm a Democrat." This information startled Clemens, and he wanted to know how the old man accounted for it. "Account for it? There ain't any accounting for it, except that if you send a damned fool to St. Louis, and you don't tell them he's a damned fool, *they'll* never find out. There's one thing sure—if I had a damned fool I should know what to do with him: ship him to St. Louis—it's the noblest market in the world for that kind of property."

Finally, Clemens slyly got around to asking the old man about himself: did he know what had happened to one Samuel Clemens. "Oh, he succeeded well enough," the man told him, "another case of a damned fool. If they'd sent him to St. Louis, he'd have succeeded sooner." To this amusing observation, Clemens concludes, "It was with much satisfaction that I recognized the wisdom of having told this candid gentleman in the beginning, that my name was Smith."[6]

One would be hard pressed to enumerate the many valuable lessons about life, docility, humility, and humor found in this short passage from *Life on the Mississippi*. No doubt the citizens of St. Louis, in the meantime, have come to discover that their greatest natural resource was explained to Samuel L. Clemens, alias Smith, by an old gentleman one Sunday morning in Hannibal, Missouri. If you send a smart young man to an Eastern college, three things may happen to him; either he will go to the dogs to die unknown in the Territories, or he will be elected to the state legislature but remain a "damned fool," or he will come back home as Mark Twain, alias Smith, enjoying a certain wisdom listening to a candid gentleman telling him he too should have been sent to St. Louis.

One final story about the life of the mind is worth recounting in this chapter. I frequently recommend to students that they should haunt used bookstores. A student I had in class a couple of years ago studied law, I think, in San Diego. He wrote that he happened to be in a used bookstore where he purchased eight books, among them a volume of Churchill's *History of England*, a book on the Goths, a biography of Dr. Johnson, and one titled *Mont-Saint-Michel and Chartres,* by none other than Henry Adams.

My young friend was delighted with the Adams book. He was especially surprised to discover what Adams had to say about Thomas Aquinas. It is with this reflection on Aquinas that I will conclude this chapter:

I was particularly taken by his [Adams's] comparison of Aquinas as a Norman to men like Abelard and Bonaventure as Bretons. The former always undertakes less than he can accomplish, but later wishes he had done more, while the latter assumes more than he can do, and later regrets it. It is difficult to look at the *Summa* of Aquinas and say, "This man undertook too little— he really ought to have been more thorough." Nevertheless, Thomas himself recognized the paucity of his own work in comparison to the Divine Perfection. This does not discourage me: I find it rather comforting that the Divine Perfection is inexhaustible to the finite human person. Boredom is hellish.

Joseph Pieper, in his book on Aquinas (*A Guide to the Summa*), says the same thing, that the *Summa* is an unfinished book. At the end of his life, Aquinas saw a vision that made him realize that in comparison to God, all he had written was but straw.

Let us end this chapter on the life of the mind, then, with the following propositions:

1. that boredom is indeed hellish;

2. that one can go to fine Eastern colleges and still return home a damned fool;

3. that nothing is on TV;

4. that the chief wonder of education is that it does not ruin everyone, teacher and taught;

5. that we do want to know the causes of things;

6. that something, at least, is true;

7. that one may be fortunate to have a tutor named Sarpedon, who is more ready to instruct than to beat his scholars;

8. that one ought to learn to waste time with your friends;

9. that some charming Lydia or handsome Linus may find one "interesting";

10. that one's souls ought not to be "flat" or one's spirit "half-hearted";

11. that one ought not to be a perfect "chucklehead," either in Hannibal or St. Louis;

12. that one must strive, for starters, to avoid the cardinal sins of pride and sloth;

13. and finally that we are blessed if, at least once in our lives, we discover "a most wonderful book," one "beyond description," and are hence incited to write its author to see if he has written anything else.

Chapter IX

The Whole Risk for a Human Being:
On the Insufficiency of Apollo

Now here, my dear Glaucon, is the whole risk for a human being, as it seems. And on this account each of us must, to the neglect of other studies, above all see to it that he is a seeker and student of that study by which he might be able to learn and find out who will give him the capacity and the knowledge to distinguish the good and the bad life, and so everywhere and always to choose the better from among those that are possible.
—Plato, *The Republic*

People wondered: where was God when the gas chambers were operating? This objection, which seemed reasonable enough before Auschwitz when one recognized all the atrocities of history, shows that in any case a purely harmonious concept of beauty is not enough. It cannot stand up to the confrontation with the gravity of the questioning about God, truth and beauty. *Apollo*, who for Plato's Socrates, was "the God" and the guarantor of unruffled beauty as "the truly divine" is absolutely no longer sufficient.
—Josef Ratzinger, "The Beauty and the Truth of Christ"

> What is it, do you think, that causes the return [to the faith]? I think it is the problem of living, for every day, every experience of evil, demands a solution. The solution is provided by the memory of the great scheme which at last we remember.
> —Hilaire Belloc, *The Path to Rome*

I

In all these chapters—on walking, on reading, on thinking, on being delighted—I have tried to recur to the theme that there are things not to be missed. The mind does have a life that is designed to be our life. Indeed, there are pleasures we should have, books we should read, walks we should take, and friends we should make. It is, however, quite possible that in the living of our lives, we may miss, even choose to miss, that which no one would really want to miss if he were really open to *what is*. In the end, the word that suffuses our life, both moral and intellectual, is *risk*. It is possible to miss that for which we have being—existence. And even if we do achieve a proper life of the mind with the final purpose of our being, it would not be significant if we could have it without our choosing it. The worthiness of our existence includes its risky-ness—its might-not-have-beenness.

One day, a student stopped me after class. He apologized for asking an "impertinent" question. I inquired about the nature of the said impertinency. I am, after all, a Thomist: "Ask and ye shall receive at least an opinion, provided you know the technical difference between opinion and truth!" The young man in fact wanted to know whether "I thought there *was* such a thing as truth" (note he did not ask whether there *was* truth, but whether I *thought* there was). Though I think such a problem as the existence of truth might, deep down, bother not a few of our kind, still it is not a question that one is asked every day. My "opinion" is that there is such a thing as truth, which, technically, means that what I hold is not just an opinion.

To my knowledge, I had never given any indication in writing or speaking that I did not hold truth to be a decided possibility, or rather to be a fact, something I hope we can still affirm today without seeming "arrogant." Thus, I was puzzled. "Why is such a question addressed to someone who obviously holds to the possibility of truth?" I have, after all, pondered with delight Aquinas's famous phrase, *omne ens est verum*, "all being is true." Josef Pieper's *The Truth of All Things* I consider to be simply a jewel of intelligence.[1] With some confidentiality, however, as if he were letting me in on some deep secret about which I was totally clueless, the student explained that, "around here and in our age groups, few people [he might have said 'no one'] think that truth exists." At this presumably startling, if not shocking, information, I did not bat an eyelash. I am a man of the world.

Surely, I thought to myself, this young man had not forgotten that I had read in class the beginning lines of Allan Bloom's *Closing of the American Mind,* in which Bloom bluntly states that the one thing any professor can be sure of, on entering a class for the first time, is that every student there thinks, or claims he thinks, that "truth is relative."[2] I will not here go into the self-contradictory irony of the "truth" of the proposition that all "truth is relative." The real iconoclasts today, young or old, are not the unbelievers in truth's existence, who are a dime a dozen, as they say, but the knowers who affirm it. I am in fact more surprised by students who do not think truth or culture is purely relative than by those who think it is.

Most students today are brought up on a steady diet of a "theory"—it is no more than that—of "tolerance" as the operative principle in all their dealings. No one wants to "judge" anything or anybody, yet, in most circumstances, that is the only intellectual operation worth performing. Such tolerance in turn is not merely a pragmatic agreement to get along even when not in intellectual harmony, something that might be defended on reasonable grounds. Rather, it is based on the idea that the only "legitimate" way we can do whatever it is we want to do is to affirm, as a general or theoretical proposition, that nothing, in principle, is or can be certain or true. Such a position frees us from all contact with reality or its having anything to say to us about *what is*.

This position was originally in Western thought an epistemological thesis about the adequacy of our senses to report external reality, whereas today it is conceived to be mostly a political or moral thesis. Any affirmation of a truth is thus considered to be "discriminatory," with tendencies to "fanaticism," the most terrible modern aberration of all. "Fanaticism," to give it its due, however, means at bottom that there are truths and they are worth affirming or pursuing, though not necessarily in just any manner. The "law" of our action or our polity under a regime of speculative and dogmatic tolerance, however, simply becomes what is enforced or accepted, with no other theoretical justification about the truth of what is affirmed. This is the theoretic background against which John Paul II called attention to the real possibility of a "democratic tyranny" *(Centesimus Annus, #46)*.

We do sense, however, that we need speculative reasons to explain or justify our practical decisions and actions, especially if we suspect that what we do is wrong by some transcendent standard—that is, if we presume we do have such a thing as a conscience. In this sense, we remain rational beings even when we implicitly reject reason in order to justify what we want and choose to do. In short, all disorder of soul seeks to defend or explain itself in terms of some apparently plausible intelligible principle or argument. The difference between being good or bad is not a difference between having an explanation and having no explanation for what we do. Rather it is between having an explanation that is logical and true and having one that is not, wherein the one that is not has enough validity to allow us to choose it for our own purposes in living as we wish. All error, in other words, as Aquinas intimated, contains some truth. The ultimate location of evil, consequently, is not in our intelligence but in our will, wherein we choose to direct ourselves through what we know either to the truth or to our own chosen version of the truth as the basis of our actions in this world.

In retrospect, I am not sure whether the young man concluded that Schall was the hopeless anachronism that everyone thought he was, or whether the young man was relieved that at least someone in his ken would, on confrontation, openly affirm the minority position that truth was indeed possible and not simply "relative." As to the issue itself, to the question, "What is truth?"—the question that Pilate ironically asked Christ at His trial—Plato's answer remains the best: to tell the truth is to affirm of *what is,* that it is, and of what is not, that it is not. Thomas Aquinas's formula is substantially the same and equally insightful: truth is the *adaequatio mentis et rei,* the conformity of the mind with reality. It is not just that there is this "conformity" (*adaequatio*) but that we know and affirm that an identity of mind and reality exists.

We know that, in knowledge, we can *be* what we are not, while remaining what we are from nature. The fact is that what is not ourselves—that is, the total complexus of other beings—can come to exist intentionally in our minds. This intentional existence is what makes it right, makes it delightful, that we are the kind of finite beings we are, beings to whom, in fact, everything is given, including the truth of things not ourselves, including indeed our very selves with our mysterious capacity to know. The doctrine of the Beatific Vision even intimates that we are finally to know God in this way—face to face.

II

I tend to conceive the young men and women whom I meet after the model of the two young potential philosophers, Adeimantus and Glaucon, in the second book of *The Republic,* though I admit that not everyone shows the zeal for truth these two young men displayed before Socrates. These young Greeks wanted to hear the truth of things presented for their understanding—in this case, the truth of justice—even when they could brilliantly and eloquently articulate the arguments against it. Yet they remained troubled and unsettled. Save us from the young men and women, or the old ones for that matter, who are never unsettled in their souls about *what is*, about reality's meaning. Adeimantus and Glaucon could not quite see why their arguments against truth or justice were wrong, even though they suspected that they were. They were unsettled in their very being because they did not know the truth.

Please God that we all find ourselves in this condition of those who know that they do not know. I love such students, such potential philosophers, as I call them. They make teaching not just a profession or a duty but an adventure. Plato himself tells them, in the seventh book of *The Republic*, that it is going to take considerable time and experience, much more than they could possibly anticipate, before they sort things out. Aristotle tells them that they will need virtue and discipline, while Aquinas tells them that they will need grace—that ultimate gift which goes against the grain of the autonomous man who is dissatisfied with everything he does not create himself. Plato, for his part, even worries that presenting the highest things to students, to potential philosophers, at too young an age will make them skeptical, for they do not yet have the full capacity and experience to know the truth. This is correct, but to be completely closed to such attractions, to such wonder about the truth of things, to such seeking, is simply to miss what it is to be a human being, particularly a young human being.

My initial point is first that we suspect that truth exists even when we cannot formulate it; and secondly, on this basis, we want to know what that truth is. *Quid sit veritas?* This relation to the truth which is at the very core of our being is the real origin of that "unsettlement" about reality that constitutes the radical dynamism in what it is to be a human being. This is what Augustine, in his *Confessions*, called—with overtones both of Plato and of Scripture—"our restless hearts." We tirelessly seek to know the truth, even when we think it does not exist or that it cannot, in principle, be known. We want to know, as Eric Voegelin puts it, the very "ground" of our finite being, since we cannot help but know that we do not cause ourselves either to be or not to be what we are.[3]

We are the "rational" beings, as Aristotle called us. Furthermore, we do not want to know this truth about ourselves for any particularly utilitarian purpose, for what we might "do" with it, though there is nothing wrong with knowing how things work, with "doing" things. In his essay, "The Sacred and 'Desacralization,'" Josef Pieper made the following remark about intellectual poverty or want, an insight concerning the ultimate non-pragmatic purpose of truth:

> At the same time that we behold this image of abundance, we must confront the image of the most radical human poverty, not material but existential want. We would be desolate if we had to live in a world containing only things which we could dispose of and use, but nothing which we could simply enjoy, without thought of any utilitarian end; a world in which there was specialized expertise, but no philosophical reflection on life as a whole.[4]

The world includes things simply to be known and enjoyed, something that can happen to the things we need and use for daily purposes. It is no accident that craftsmen not only make tools, but beautiful tools. But beauty does not add to the usefulness of a tool.

Thus, we just want to know the truth. We are the kind of beings who, even in conditions of perfect abundance, as in the Garden of Eden (the original "image of abundance"), remain unsettled. We are unsettled simply because we do not know and know that we do not know. The famous temptation to "be like gods" comes with our very existence in the midst, not of want, but of abundance. Most of the world's skeptics live in societies of abundance and in institutions with large libraries.

Adam and Eve, we might say, experienced, to use Pieper's word, "existential want." Or perhaps I should say, at the core of our being we always reach a point where we have to decide whether the truth that we seek exists in *what is* or whether we make the truth ourselves in conformity not to *what is* but to what we would prefer it to be, as if it were up

to ourselves to create ourselves from nothing. The real division of mankind, and probably of the universe, passes through this question of
whether *what is* is something of our own making or whether it is something we receive as already made to be *what it is*—and indeed, in being
what it is, to be best for us also.

The worst life that we can imagine, in one sense, to borrow Pieper's
trenchant phrase again, "is one containing no philosophical reflection
on life as a whole." To engage in philosophy, Leo Strauss observed, is to
seek a knowledge of the whole, as if somehow it is ours to know. The
Christian gloss on this definition of philosophy is to accept all the help
we can get to obtain this "knowledge of the whole," even if it is given us
by revelation. Ultimately, we have to ask ourselves whether we want to
know only what it is in our capacity to know or whether we also can
accept a gift of knowledge that would lead us to the whole which is not
of our own making.

III

Years ago, when I was still a relatively young man—a period that my
students today refer to as "ancient history"—I read a passage in Hilaire
Belloc's wonderful book *The Path to Rome*, a passage that has always
haunted me somehow. It immediately follows the introductory observation of Belloc that I cited above, wherein he reflects that it is our
regular encounter with living, with evil itself, that eventually recalls to
us a scheme of things that we once knew. This scheme, the structure of
our faith itself, describes to us how things fit together, the good over
against the evil—how things that stand out of nothingness simply *are*.

The passage that I recall is of remarkable pertinence, I think, especially to the condition of Catholicism in our time and place: Those
who have wandered away from the faith and return, Belloc rightly reflected, obviously recalling his own memories, "suffer hard things." He
finds a "gulf" between himself, as one of those who had once wandered, and his "many companions." He proceeds to explain what he

means: "We are perpetually thrust into minorities, and the world almost begins to talk a strange language; we are troubled by the human machinery of a perfect and supernatural revelation; we are over-anxious for its safety, alarmed, and in danger of violent decisions."[5]

"Violent decisions" seem to be at hand, and we indeed talk a strange language. I read during Christmas the account of a school district that does not even allow the word "Christmas" to be pronounced in any classroom. Justice Holmes, in a famous decision, once said we are not allowed to shout "fire" in a crowded theater. Evidently, today the word "Christmas" substitutes for the word "fire" among the words we cannot speak, as does the word "sin." Christianity is indeed sometimes pictured as "a fire on the earth." In the name of toleration theory, it supposedly makes no difference what forms our souls. Yet we seek to remove from our souls those traditions which called our attention to the fact that we have souls in the first place. Tolerance does not tolerate truth, though that was once its purpose, the finding of truth.

We are indeed "troubled," to put it mildly, over the "human machinery of a perfect and supernatural revelation." We think of bankrupt dioceses. A cousin of mine in Colorado told me that two neighbors across the street told her that they stopped going to church because of the ecclesiastical scandals. My brother-in-law told me of a Presbyterian lady who assumed that the scandals had "disproved" the Catholic Church, and proceeded to invite him to join a local church that had ten ministers—eight of whom, including the pastor, were women. This latter statistic, fortunately, confirmed his life-long devotion to Catholicism.

Others, including a colleague of mine, are not so much shocked by the facts of degradation but rather by how little and how slowly anything has been done about them, even at the highest levels. We worried about why Pope John Paul II himself had been so reticent, so apparently uncertain or unable to act firmly and decisively with men, whom he himself appointed to high office, when they failed him. A priest told me that two of his friends in Boston were afraid or ashamed to wear the Roman collar in the streets.

IV

The Holocaust, as Josef Cardinal Ratzinger, now Pope Benedict XVI, once remarked, again forced us to attend to the question of how a good God could allow these terrible things. Historian that he is, Ratzinger reminds us that this crime was not the first time in history that such an accusation against God was founded on a reaction to human atrocities. Many people who read the Old Testament itself, moreover, are particularly bothered by what looks like God actually approving and encouraging the slaughter of innocents, women and children and the elderly. A Jesuit friend, now dead, once told me that he would not read the Old Testament because it was so bloody. Evidently, if he had written it, it would be un-bloody; that is, it would not have been what was given to us. But with the current child-abuse scandals, the problem is not so much, "Why did God allow such atrocities?"—itself not a new question—but rather, "Why did so many clerics participate in them?"

Belloc's *The Path to Rome* is about a walk he took in 1901, a year after the death of Nietzsche. Nietzsche, in a famous book, tried to get "beyond good and evil," which "getting beyond" is indeed one way of confronting the problem, provided of course that there is some "beyond" that is itself neither good nor evil. It is interesting in this current case that secularists, who profess to see little wrong with much of this activity when considered in the abstract, are themselves scandalized when clerics do not practice what they preach. It reminds us of Chesterton's remark that secularists are more scandalized when clerics do observe their vows than when they do not. Sin is ultimately less interesting than virtue, let alone grace.

At the beginning of the twentieth century, Belloc already was worried about precisely "the human machinery" of supernatural revelation.[6] Why ever would God not only create a world in which terrible evils exist, but also institute a church whose leaders turned out, too many times, to be sinners? God's "ways are not our ways," as it says in Isaiah. Our complaints against God reveal our conception of God. We think He should do what we would do in His position. We, with our notions of fairness and justice, would not have allowed these things to happen, or so we surmise, without reflecting on just what we would have had to do to stop them. Granted these facts of disorder in high places, we can either reject God as unworthy of us, or suspect that there is something more profound in God's ways than we are willing to suspect. Had God given us a sinless clergy, He would have no doubt also given us, simultaneously, religious figures who could not understand our own sins. If history attested to no holocausts, it probably could attest to no free will either.

I am reminded of these popular and contemporary questions not merely because they concern us all and are part of the quest for the meaning of things in which we are all involved, but also because they are issues already anticipated in revelation and in our reflection on it. The demand for a world in which there was no possibility of atrocities or for a church in which the hierarchy was sinless might be conceivable. Indeed, it was conceived, by God, in the Garden of Eden, as Genesis tells us. But if such a world existed, we can be sure that we would not exist, for we are a product of a world in which atrocities are possible and a sinful clergy is too often a fact. The question is not whether God might not have created some other sinless or atrocity-free world, but whether He could have created the world in which we live and still be God.

V

The penultimate sentence in the introduction to James Thurber's autobiography, *My Life and Hard Times*, reads, "It is unfortunate . . . that even a well-ordered life can not lead anybody safely around the inevitable doom that waits in the skies."[7] This passage, both amusing and profound in its context, is but another way of stating Socrates' notion that philosophy is basically a preparation for death. Socrates said in *The Apology* that nothing bad can happen to a good man, for even death is not known to be bad, while doing wrong is evil in all cases. We are aware not only that the good can suffer—"the inevitable doom that waits in the skies" is not to be avoided—but also that their suffering and their doom is an argument for, not against, a "well-ordered life."

We are reminded from time to time, especially by the classical authors, that the very being of a human person involves a "risk." We are to be "seekers." Built into the very structure of our being is the question of what is it all about. And the fact that we are "seekers" and not, in the first instance, "knowers," causes us to wonder if there is anyone who can give us the "capacity" and the "knowledge" to distinguish between what Socrates called "the good and the bad life." Once we have learned to distinguish between these two sorts of lives, we still must "choose" from among those lives that are "possible" to us. The risk or drama of human existence does not seem to arise over the question of whether something is offered to us, but whether on its being offered, we accept or reject it.

In St. Augustine's commentary on Psalm 109 (Wednesday of the second week of Advent), we read:

> God, who is faithful, put himself in our debt, not by receiving anything but by promising so much. A promise was not sufficient for him; he chose to commit himself in writing as well, as it were making a contract of his promises. He wanted us to be able to see the way in which his promises were redeemed when he began to discharge them. And so the time of the prophets . . . a foretelling of the promises. He promised eternal salvation, everlasting happiness with the angels, an immortal inheritance, endless glory, the joyful vision of his face, his holy dwelling in heaven, and after the resurrection from the dead, no further fear of dying.

If indeed we choose "not to be good," we do so generally under the aegis of an alternative theory of what good means. We dispute what the good is, seeking ourselves to formulate its meaning. That is, we put ourselves in the position of the gods; we make ourselves the cause of the distinctions in things. If we argue that God, not ourselves, is responsible for the well-known evils that we all seem to recognize, we have to be careful what we propose. If the evil in the world is caused by God, then I suppose we have to reject God and build another world. In fact, this is what we may very well be trying to do. On the other hand, if evil has origins in our own will, then the cure for the world's ills would seem to be to acknowledge a good that we did not ourselves create. We probably cannot have it both ways. And that, in essence, constitutes the risk of our own existence.

When Josef Ratzinger remarked that the serene beauty of Apollo is not sufficient for us, he did not mean to chastise the Greek philosophers, poets, and dramatists. They did discover something worthy that moves our soul. Beauty does astonish us. But beauty in a world with tragedy, with wanton evil, caused by those whom God created to choose the good and the beautiful, does not allow us to escape the Crucifixion. Our concept of beauty—and we should have a concept of beauty—ought not to be such that we do not, mentally at least, allow the world that exists to be. If we want our ways to be God's ways, we will certainly end up with a different kind of world than the one we have. The question must always be, is our world an improvement? I like to ask this question because it states baldly the real issue: namely, does the fact of human sin and disorder imply, logically, that this particular world in which we exist ought not to exist in the first place? Would nothingness be better than an existing world in which terrible things not only can happen but have happened, even in our own lives?

The brief answer to this perplexing question is that the glory and beauty of God remain the same whether we exist or not. God needs us not. But assuming that God can choose to have something exist outside of Himself, it follows that the greater glory would be if creatures existed which could acknowledge and love *what is*, and to say of *what is*, that it is. This position would intrinsically mean that creatures could prefer themselves to God, otherwise they would not be real. If this be true, we should not expect that our existence would not include things that go terribly wrong. We leave God in only one position. Sometimes it is called bringing "good" out of "evil." In reality, what God does is carry forth to its proper end whatever good exists wherever it is found, even in sin. No sin takes place without its being based on some good. The history of the world, including the ecclesiastical world, including our own personal world, is the working out of this drama of how we choose and how God continues to bring things to glory in spite of any formal rejection of his Beauty.

In an old *Peanuts* series titled "Here Comes Charlie Brown," I came across the following scene: Charlie and Lucy are walking in what looks to be a wintry countryside. Lucy has a pout on her face. Innocently, Charlie asks her, "Are you going to make any New Year's Resolutions, Lucy?" The next scene is unexpectedly explosive. We see Charlie being completely flipped over, as Lucy shouts at him, "What? What for?! What's wrong with me now? I LIKE MYSELF JUST THE WAY I AM!" Charlie manages to upright himself, but Lucy continues yelling even more vehemently, "WHY SHOULD I CHANGE?! WHAT IN THE WORLD IS THE MATTER WITH YOU, CHARLIE BROWN!" In the last scene, Lucy is still yelling, now with her fists raised to the heavens, "I am all right the way I am! I don't have to improve! How? I ask you, How?" Finally, we see a thoroughly defeated Charlie Brown slinking away and muttering to himself, "Good grief!"[8]

If we reflect on this scene, we must acknowledge that in a very real sense, Lucy is indeed all right "the way she is." That is, her very being is good and will remain so. When she asks "how" she can improve *what she is*, we must confess that she cannot. But Charlie is also correct. The drama of our existence does not consist in the fact that we are born, but in the actions that flow from our being. Our resolutions imply that we can change our ways; indeed, they imply that at times we must change our ways. But we need not. If it is not overly irreverent, I would say that part of the enjoyment of God's being God is the delight He must take in countering our actions with our being created good. No evil simply sits there. Its consequences themselves constitute the drama of reality, not only in our own lives, but in those affected by our sins and, to be sure, by our good deeds.

The whole risk of being a human being is that we do not know, that we do not choose that great scheme in which all that we know and do takes place. Who will indeed, as Plato asked, give us "the capacity and the knowledge to distinguish the good and the bad life?" The life of the mind is the arena in which the risk of our existence is known, known even by us. We sometimes forget, indeed we sometimes never know that, at bottom, the life of one's mind depends on one's philosophy, a theme to which we turn in the final chapter.

Chapter X

ON THE THINGS THAT DEPEND ON PHILOSOPHY

[I]t is not unusual to meet people who think that not to believe in any truth, or not to adhere firmly to any assertion as unshakeably true in itself, is a primary condition required of democratic citizens in order to be tolerant of one another and to live in peace with one another. May I say that these people are in fact the most intolerant people, for if perchance they were to believe in something as unshakeably true, they would feel compelled, by the same stroke, to impose by force and coercion their own belief on their co-citizens. The only remedy they have found to get rid of their abiding tendency to fanaticism is to cut themselves off from truth.

—Jacques Maritain, *Heroic Democracy*

Some dogmas, we are told, were credible in the twelfth century, but are not credible in the twentieth. You might as well say that a certain philosophy can be believed on Mondays, but cannot be believed on Tuesdays. You might as well say of a view of the cosmos that it was suitable to half-past three, but not suitable to half-past four. What a man can believe depends upon his philosophy, not upon the clock or the century. If a man believes in unalterable natural law, he cannot believe in any miracle in any age. If a man believes in will behind law, he can believe in any miracle in any age.

—G. K. Chesterton, *Orthodoxy*

I

What can it mean to suggest that some things "depend" on philosophy? And what things might these be? Philosophy, after all, is "for its own sake." Philosophers, moreover, even in classical times, were considered to be rather odd or eccentric. To "depend" on them was, to say the least, quite rash. Even St. Paul associated philosophy with "foolishness." In Athens, it was said to be difficult to distinguish the philosopher from the fool. To the normal man, midway between philosopher and fool, both seemed to be distinctly peculiar. The life of the mind, however, flourishes when it strives to explain the *things that are.*

Yet this same "normal man" who might greet the professional philosopher with suspicion must also himself be considered to be a philosopher, to be interested in philosophic things, though he may not call them by that noble name. Revelation seems corrective of philosophy on this score. Revelation purports to identify several basic things that the philosophers only hint at. It is concerned both with the intelligence and with the destiny of everyone. John Paul II, in *Fides et Ratio*, put it well:

> The truths of philosophy . . . are not restricted only to the sometimes ephemeral teachings of professional philosophers. All men and women . . . are in some sense philosophers and have their own philosophical conceptions with which they direct their lives. In one way or another, they shape a comprehensive vision and an answer to the question of life's meaning and in the light of this they interpret their own life's course and regulate their behavior. (#30)

There was a time in our culture when we spoke of familiar figures like the "gentleman doctor," "gentleman lawyer," or "gentleman farmer." The American founding fathers, indeed, were usually both gentlemen lawyers and gentlemen farmers. Benjamin Rush was a gentleman doctor who began as a gentleman lawyer. The noble notions of "gentleman" or "gentlewoman" that we associate with Burke, Newman, and Samuel Johnson have become less intelligible to us. In an egalitarian age, everyone is a gentleman, no matter what their manners or tastes. Legally, even "barbarians" are "gentlemen." It sometimes seems that everyone is also becoming a lawyer. Josef Pieper, however, wrote,

> In Plato, there is a concept of slavery which no social changes, no emancipation of the slaves, can wipe off the face of the earth. This conception is rooted in the belief that what is truly human is never the average. The standard by which truth and falsehood, good and evil, are measured, is not alone the divine, but also the human. To put that more exactly: the standard is what man himself is capable of being, and what he is called upon to be.[1]

The average and the excellent are not the same thing even in a fallen world in which everyone is not expected to be perfect. Both the ordinary man and the philosopher, it seems, because of their common humanity, have a need of something beyond philosophy: redemption, perhaps.

Such expressions of a more excellent way of being *what one is* were, however, designed to suggest that "ordinary" doctors or lawyers (or, as we will see in appendix III, clerics) were not, as such, "gentleman" lawyers or doctors. Moreover, the gentleman doctor or lawyer was not the same as the man exclusively "learned in the law or medicine." The specialist, the one who had taken the time to learn more and more about a particular discipline, was not what was meant by the "gentleman" lawyer or doctor. A certain unsettlement of the soul accompanied knowing so much about so relatively little. Somehow there was a wisdom beyond, but not exclusive of, one's profession.

"Gentlemen" were so designated because they were wisely learned or cultured beyond their own professions. They actually read poetry and history. They knew about Nietzsche as well as St. Bernard. They might play the cello or write short stories. They played golf or handball. Being skilled or learned in a given profession was considered by them to not be enough for a complete life no matter how worthy the occupation. Those who only knew their own area of expertise were practitioners, journeymen, or masters, to use the medieval terms. The gentleman lawyer or doctor not only knew where his own profession fit into the scheme of things, but he was also interested in the very scheme of things itself.

Plato often refers to the fact that the doctor's craft, as craft, is limited by what it is to be healthy, something the doctor does not create but only serves. Once a person is healthy, the doctor's task is over. A doctor, as a human being, must live, and live well, among the many who are not sick. The great human question is not how to make us healthy, however important that may be, but what to "do" when we are already healthy. Health addresses health, as Aristotle put it. When we are healthy, we pay little attention to our bodies' workings. Rather we want to know and to act in a world of incredible abundance and variety.

In *The Republic*, Socrates refers to the case of a certain Herodicus, a physician trainer—a sort of team doctor, I suppose. This good man spent his whole life tending to his own health. The result was that he stretched out his death into "a lengthy process." He could not cure himself; "he lived out his life under medical treatment, with no leisure for anything else whatever. If he departed even a little from his accustomed regimen, he became completely worn out, but because his [medical] skill made dying difficult, he lived into old age" (406a–b). Absent a Christian sense of the value of suffering, this sort of leisureless life was thought to be rather fruitless, since it participated in none of the activities of leisure for which we are originally intended. Life is not merely about staying alive. What do we do when all else is done is a philosophic question of great significance.

Moreover, very few if any human beings can really be specialists or skilled in more than one or two areas or sub-areas. The list of specialties under, say, tax law alone approaches infinity. No doubt, we live in a world in which we need many skills in all areas of life so that we might be skilled in our own field without losing the advantage of participating in the goods with which other specialists present us. Understanding this need is what stands behind the notion of precisely a "common" good, a notion thought to encompass both the general good and particular goods. The novelist Walker Percy, a gentleman doctor if there ever was one, once remarked in an interview:

> What I was protesting . . . was the view of so many, not merely scientists, but also writers and artists, that only scientists and only science is interested in telling the truth. Provable, demonstrable truth, whereas art and writing have to do with play, feeding the emotions, entertainment. I've always held that art and even novels are just as valid as science, just as cognitive. In fact, I see my own writing as not really a great departure from my original career, science and medicine, because . . . where science will bring you to a certain point and no further, it can say nothing about what a man is or what he must do.[2]

Such reflections obviously emanate from a man unsettled by the narrowness of his profession. Percy mistrusts a scientific philosophy that prevents his mind from dealing with truth wherever it is found. He is concerned about methods or epistemologies that do not, by their own structures, allow truth to be found at all.

II

Boswell tells us that in the spring of 1768 he had published his book about Corsica. He then returned to London, only to discover that Samuel Johnson was in Oxford with his friend Mr. Chambers, who had become Vinerian Professor at New Inn Hall. On arriving at Oxford and being treated with gentility by Mr. Chambers, Boswell inquired of Johnson, in his capacity as "a moralist," whether "the practice of law, in some degree, hurt the nice feeling of honesty." Recall that Boswell himself was a lawyer. The gist of Johnson's reply was, "Why no, Sir, if you act properly. You are not to deceive your clients with false representations of your opinion: you are not to tell lies to a judge."[3] Boswell's question obviously implies that, in the practice of law, one might well be tempted to misrepresent one's opinion to clients or to tell lies to judges, in short to "hurt the nice feeling of honesty" that presumably every man should have, lawyer or not. The lawyer, Johnson implied, is already involved in philosophic questions by his very profession.

The question of the "use" of philosophy, of whether philosophy, in other words, is, as many suspect, "useless," is itself a question of philosophy. It is of some importance to know if our solicitor thinks it legitimate to lie to us, his clients. Yet the pages of Plato abound with adversarial suspicions that the answer to the question of whether philosophy is "useful" is negative. The philosopher, as we have indicated, is popularly looked upon as a rather tweedy, odd character, hardly capable of negotiating his way down the street. Among the masses who observe him he is a subject of much humor and pleasantry.

Even Socrates portrayed himself, at the beginning of his trial, as someone who had not been much concerned with public or practical affairs. He claimed to have little clue about how to present himself before the law. "Gentlemen, if you hear me making my defense in the same kind of language as I am accustomed to use in the marketplace by the bankers' tables, where many of you have heard me, and elsewhere, do not be surprised or create a disturbance on that account. The position is this: this is my first appearance in a law court, at the age of seventy; I am therefore simply a stranger to the manner of speaking here" (17c–d). Socrates in fact did not succeed in defending himself before the Athenian court, though his trial still goes on in our books if we read them, as we should. Judged by its external consequences, philosophy appeared to be rather useless to Socrates, however eloquent to us his speech before the law court now appears to be.

Nonetheless, philosophy has always prided itself on being "beyond use." The life of the mind is worth fostering, it claims, for its own sake. We want it for no other purpose but itself. Indeed, we want other things for it, for philosophy, not the other way around. Through it, we know where things, including ourselves, belong in the order of the cosmos. Even if philosophy had no "use," we would still want to possess it. It is one of those things which, after it has been proved to be good for nothing further, we still want. Utility—the asking, "Is it useful?"—is itself a consideration of moral philosophy, one of the "goods" to which we can legitimately tend, but not necessarily the highest one. The subject of utility is taken up in Aristotle's *Ethics* (1156a22 ff.) and Cicero's *De Officiis*.

Every day we are surrounded by things that are merely useful, but still we are glad that we have them; the hammer to pound the nail, the razor to shave our beard, even perhaps law courts, to render what is "due" to us. But the elevation of "utility" to the highest consideration of philosophy in the nineteenth century (the Epicureans had already done something similar in ancient times) has not been particularly "useful" either to politics or to philosophy, though it has provided occasion to clarify exactly what we mean by the usefulness of something. Paradoxically, "utility," as a philosophy, is not useful. A universe of utility is a universe with no real meaning. One dubious attraction of a philosophy that logically makes the world meaningless, however, is that it exempts us from responsibility and allows us to do what we will.

Christoph Cardinal von Schönborn once remarked that Thomas Aquinas was the first man who was ever canonized simply for thinking. What else can this affirmation mean except that thinking in itself is a worthy activity? Indeed, it is the activity that most distinguishes us as human. The opposite of thinking is not "not to think at all." The opposite of thinking rightly is thinking wrongly. While it is true that we praise the being who has the natural capacity to think, what is important about thinking is not the faculty or process of thinking, but what is concluded, what is thought about, the truth that is affirmed.

We are interested in Thomas Aquinas, therefore, not because he had a mind, or because his mind worked like all human minds work, but because of what he thought with his mind. The life of the mind is ultimately concerned with truth. We are concerned with the truth that Aquinas affirmed, a truth we too, if we follow him, come to reaffirm through reading him. We are interested in what he said about the soul, virtue, law, metaphysics, and God. Truth is not Aquinas's truth, even when he is the one who leads us to see that something is true. Truth cannot, as such, be "owned" by anyone. It is free and freeing. But the "freedom" of truth is not the power to make it into its opposite and still call it true.

"Every demonstrable proposition is, *de jure*, communicable without limits," Yves Simon wrote concerning truth's solidity:

> But it often happens that the understanding of a fully demonstrated proposition or even that of an immediately obvious one, requires conditions which are not commonly satisfied in any society. *De jure* some propositions of metaphysics and ethics are no less communicable than any theorem of geometry or law of biology. At philosophical conventions deaf men make speeches for other deaf men, and blind men play pantomimes for other blind men, and this will never prove anything against the intrinsic communicability of philosophic truth.[4]

To use Platonic terms, truth is to say of *what is* that it is, of what is not, that it is not. We are given minds precisely to make such affirmations. We have a longing to know precisely the truth and cannot be settled with anything less. A mind that cannot or will not make an affirmation or judgment is not a mind.

The world's worst tyrants were often men of thought—not just brutes, as we sometimes think. As the Greek writers depicted them, they were often handsome, charming, and witty. The difference between the philosopher-king and the tyrant was not that one thought and the other did not. The tyrant had intellectual capacities every bit as great and powerful as the greatest philosopher. That was why he was so dangerous. Indeed, it was often his philosophy that compelled the tyrant into politics. The tyrant differed from the philosopher because of what he willed, not because of any native difference in intellectual ability.

III

A city, to be a city, with its variety of things to be done and goods to be exchanged, cannot be composed solely of philosophers (or tyrants), at least if we assume that philosophers are specialists who devote their whole lives to their unusual trade. Philosophers are not shoemakers or airline pilots, though we might well expect, in their own ways, that shoemakers and airline pilots know something of philosophy, of the truth of things. If, however, an airline pilot is, philosophically, a pessimist who has published books on the virtues of suicide or on the political value of terrorism, if he is someone who does not think that life is worth living, we do well to take another flight. Here is at least one case where philosophy might be rather "useful" indeed.

Socrates proceeded, after prodding the young potential philosophers Adeimantus and Glaucon, to build a city in speech in order to find how injustice arose. He next proposed, as a building block, a principle of specialization, whereby each member of the city was to be free to devote himself to what was most fitting for him to do (369a–c). This separate contribution of each was not seen as a principle of absolute separation or isolation, but rather of cooperation. Most worthy things need time and talent to come to fruition. "And because people need many things and because one person calls on a second out of one need and on a third out of a different need," Socrates continued, "many people gather in a single place to live together as partners and helpers. And such a settlement is called a city. Isn't that so? . . . And if they share things with one another, giving and taking, they do so because each believes that this is better for himself" (369b–c). It is better for oneself that one is not required to do everything; otherwise one would obtain very little of anything compared to the abundance of what one might have with the help of others. "Man is by nature a political animal," as Aristotle put it in making this same point.

The common good also includes, as it were, our private good, as Socrates implied. Indeed, as the Athenian says in *The Laws*, "the proper object of true political skill is not the interest of private individuals but the common good. This is what knits the state together, whereas private interests make it disintegrate. If the public interest is well served, rather than the private, then the individual and the community alike are benefited" (875a–b). The philosopher is the one who knows this common good as precisely common, as making the private goods also to be what they are. The common good is not some sort of overarching alien good separate and distinct from the reality of private goods.

This principle of specialization has been articulated in many forms throughout history. In Pius XI's famous encyclical *Quadragesimo Anno* (1931), it was called the principle of subsidiarity (#79–80). Yves Simon, in his *General Theory of Authority*, called it the principle of "autonomy"— "by the principle of autonomy; any pursuit that a particular unit is able to carry out satisfactorily ought to be entrusted to precisely such a unit."[5] On the political level, arrangements like federalism and confederation have likewise sought to preserve this twofold advantage, the participation in a larger good while retaining the value of the smaller unit both for its members and for the excellence of the product. In order for the whole to be the whole, the parts must be the parts. Or to put it another way, the preservation of the parts is itself one of the main functions of common authority. The collapse of parts with their own relative autonomy brings about tyrannical uniformity.

IV

The main purpose of philosophy insofar as it is political philosophy is the work of persuasion—for this is the way philosophy must proceed, its main and really only weapon. Who is persuading whom? The lesson of both the trial of Socrates and the trial of Christ is that the city can kill the philosopher, if it chooses to do so. It always has the necessary raw power. The philosopher's ultimate protection, then, lies in what he thinks about death, as Socrates put it at his trial. Most often cities choose the actions they will put into effect within their limits through the form of laws and their execution. As in the case of Socrates before his Athenian accusers and in the case of Christ before Pilate or Caiphas, the question arises whether the politician is persuadable, open to listen to and follow the philosopher. If he is not, the philosopher is dead. His death, insofar as we attend to it, is what subsequently states his case before the witnessing of mankind.

The significant difference between the two rather similar Platonic characters Thrasymachus in *The Republic* and Callicles in the *Gorgias* has to do with how they listened to the philosopher. Thrasymachus held, much in advance of Machiavelli, the notion that justice is power—the interest of the strongest. However, the result of his discussion with Socrates in the first book of *The Republic* was that he had no more arguments to defend his own position. Thus, reluctantly, he saw that he could not hold it and became in turn rather friendly toward Socrates. In this case, the philosopher moved the politician, or at least the sophist.

Callicles, on the other hand, never seriously discusses the question of whether philosophy is important to the politician. Philosophy is merely something we amusingly study in college but quickly put aside when we come to exercise actual power. When, in the course of his conversation with Socrates, Callicles sees that he cannot defend his own view, he refuses to continue the conversation. Conversation is the only weapon of the philosopher against the politician. When the politician refuses to continue any discussion about the rightness of his procedures or ideas, we know that the philosopher is dead, though we don't know whether death is the final word even for the politician. That he suspected it was not constituted the content of the last book of Plato's *Republic,* wherein the question of ultimate rewards and punishments comes up.

Thus it is that the possibility of philosophy to some extent depends on the success of the political philosopher in directly or indirectly rendering the actual politician benevolent. This approach does not deny that politicians are basically suspicious, and sometimes rightly so, of the possibility of the philosopher undermining the moral foundations of the polity, of the existing city's explanation of itself to itself. The experienced politician, at his peril, must understand the damage caused by unworthy philosophers in the city. In Greek thought and history, Alcibiades, the most charming of the tyrants and of the young men around Socrates, serves forever as the symbol of the validity of this concern. And we should not forget, following the *Symposium,* that Alcibiades was even the most dangerous threat to the integrity of Socrates, or of philosophy itself. Both the philosopher and the politician who do not love truth after their own lights are dangerous to philosophy and to the city, indeed even to themselves.

Thanks to Plato, we know that philosophy does not always succeed in convincing the politicians to let the philosopher live. But, philosophy can still flourish. Had Socrates, instead of drinking the hemlock according to the law, chosen banishment instead, or to cease to philosophize, or to escape from jail, as he was free to do, philosophy would not have triumphed. Many a "philosopher" who ends up violating the Socratic principle that "it is never right to do wrong" drops into obscurity. Others become infamous.

V

Following a remark of Chesterton, I have titled this final chapter on the life of the mind "On the Things That Depend on Philosophy." For it is by our philosophy that we see the world, not by our eyes, unless our eyes themselves are directed by a philosophy that affirms *what is*. We can divert both our eyes and our minds from seeing what is there, what is to be seen or known. Whether a philosophy is true or not does not depend on whether it is ancient or modern, whether it is from this land or that, or whether it is Monday or Tuesday. It depends on its understanding of things, on its willingness to be measured by things of which it is not itself the cause.

Does democracy, does a legal system, depend on a philosophy that affirms that the truth can be known? Let us suppose, for the sake of argument, that democracy does depend on a philosophical position that specifically denies that truth is possible, indeed that affirms that truth is dangerous in politics, if not in life itself. In an obvious sense, of course, truth has always been considered to be dangerous, specifically to falsity. Truth and falsity themselves belong to a philosophical system that maintains that they are not the same, even when there is a disagreement about what specific thing might be true and what false. Part of the purpose of both philosophy and polity is to find this out—what is true and what is not. The "truth" that there is no "truth" founds all skepticism and grounds it in incoherence.

Within the philosophical system that, as part of its own tenets, denies that truth is possible in order to suggest that all things are possible, the major danger is any view that maintains that "absolute truths" exist and can be known. Generally, this latter position is said to be "fanatical." Thus, one who holds that truth is to say of *what is* that it is, and of what is not that it is not, is deemed a fanatic. Proponents of this view use their minds to deny the purpose of mind, which is to affirm the truth of things. Evidently, the philosophic view that there is no truth is held to be a conclusion that is necessary in order to reject other positions. What other positions? Those that recognize that there is error and evil that have to be identified and acknowledged as precisely what they are, evils and errors. Tolerance as a "theoretic" philosophic position means that any philosophy that recognizes that, in the order of things—including human things—there are things wrong or evil, is by definition false and dangerous.

However, if there is a position that allows people to live at peace with one another yet does not involve the denial of the possibility of truth, the presumed alternative, "either no truth or no democracy," would be false. What is interesting about the remarks of Maritain that I have cited at the beginning of this chapter is his awareness that the theory of tolerance that sees itself only as based on the denial of truth is itself a "fanaticism." It refuses to admit the validity of arguments about the truth.

The logic of this remark is worth spelling out: since one cannot conceive a theory in which people of different persuasions can tolerate each other, then in order to make no theory dangerous to another, one must deny that any theory is true. As Maritain pointed out, such a view understands truth only as something that, if it exists, "must" be imposed. The proponents of this position, in self-defense, deny that there is any truth possible on any terms to anybody, and that this fact is the foundation of democracy. Such a view of democracy, then, results not from a surfeit of philosophy but from a lack of it.

This observation brings us back to the question of what philosophy is and where it can exist Clearly, existing polities can embrace, as the foundation of their laws, that there is no truth. This is the truth that they hold as "self-evident." Therefore, all things are permitted. If anything is not permitted, it is not because there is anything objectionable about it with regard to truth, but simply that the polity wills it to be so. Some other polity, with equal logic, may will the opposite.

Usually, the view that all is permitted is modified by the notion that what "harms" others is not permitted. If we have a "right" to do something, it would seem that others have an obligation to allow us to exercise that right. This is particularly the case if our rights, as often conceived today, are based on nothing but an arbitrary decision or a law that admittedly has no truth as its foundation. Ironically, this view that all is permitted, combined with the notion of "harm," has worked to expand the powers of the state, not to lessen them. The state in such a world now has no theoretic limits to its competence.

Remember what Chesterton said: "What a man can believe depends on his philosophy, not on the clock or the century." Within all professions—law, medicine, clergy, farming, education, politics, business, craftsmanship—there is a need for those who are also devoted to *what is*. Philosophers are not the only ones affected by answers to philosophical questions. Indeed, the very existence of revelation suggests that not even philosophy can answer all philosophic questions. In the course of his short active life of about twenty-five years, Thomas Aquinas is said to have asked some ten thousand questions. What is significant about Aquinas is not that he asked so many questions, but that he also answered them. That is what the life of the mind is about. If philosophy is a quest, it is also a search for answers. It does not depend on the time or the century.

Let me, finally, recall these principles:

1. "What is truly human is never the average."

2. "You are not to tell lies to the judge."

3. "At philosophical conventions deaf men make speeches for other deaf men."

4. Science "can say nothing about what a man is or what he must do."

5. "The truths of philosophy . . . are not restricted to the sometimes ephemeral teachings of the professional philosophers."

6. "The standard by which truth and falsity, good and evil, are measured, is not alone the divine, but also the human."

7. What is significant about Aquinas is not that he *asked* ten thousand questions, but that he *answered* them.

8. *What we can believe does indeed depend on our philosophy.* This is what the life of the mind is about.

Conclusion

THE THINGS THE MIND DID NOT MAKE

> There is a whole problem of the human mind, which is necessarily concerned with the things that it did not make; with the things that it could not make; including itself.
>
> —G. K. Chesterton, "Our Birthday"

The life of the mind is filled with discoveries of things it did not itself make. It is all right to be a human being, because what is not ourselves is capable of being ours while remaining itself. This is what it means to have a mind alive to things. We can "live" or "be" what we are not because we have minds. But in so doing, we, happily, remain ourselves. Indeed, we are more ourselves. I have always been struck by exhortations to be virtuous, to "do good and avoid evil." This is the first practical principle that we come to understand upon seeing that being—*what is*—can be desired. The good is, after all, what exists seen under the aspect of its desirability. The *things that are* are worthy. All things are created good. *Omne ens est bonum.*

The "splendor of discovery" is a phrase that I am quite fond of, even though it is not mine. I think that I like it precisely because it is not mine. I like to live in a world in which others, even others I do not know, have already seen something I have not yet seen. I like the idea that teachers can bring me to a place where I too can see the point of a thing, see it by myself, but only because someone else took the trouble to orient me in the right direction.

We have all had the experience of someone saying to us, "Don't you see?" Suppose we are looking across a river to a building or tree on the other bank. At first, we cannot make it out. Our friend is impatient with us; "Don't you see?" And suddenly, if we focus correctly, we see what is being pointed out to us. "Yes, now I see!" (*Now I See* was the title of a book by the English sportsman and philosopher Arnold Lunn. It is still a good book.) The phrase "now I see" captures the drama of our existence. We are not just concerned with "doing" something, but also with understanding. Nothing is really complete unless it is also understood.

The word "discovery" has entered my own philosophic vocabulary for another reason. In his introduction to Vincent McNabb's *The Catholic Church and Philosophy*, Hilaire Belloc, our friend with whom we have walked in these pages if for no other reason than to help us see the things that are there, gave the following definition of philosophy: "Philosophy signifies primarily the love of knowledge—ultimate knowledge upon the ultimate realities, and, by extension, it especially signifies the solving of questions which the mind puts to itself relative to the most important subjects with which the mind can deal." The mind puts questions to itself. It does not hesitate to ask about the "most important subjects with which the mind can deal." I sometimes think that we are afraid to ask such questions. In *The Republic*, Glaucon is called "brave" by Socrates because he had the courage to ask ultimate questions even when he was not sure that they had any answer, or that they had an answer that was really worthy of our lot, or, more dangerously, that they had an answer he could accept.

It is in this context that Belloc also used the term "discovery." One of the major excitements of being a human being is precisely to discover what has been already discovered. Belloc's friend Chesterton talks of the remarkable experience of setting out in the world to find a promised land. When it is found, when we finally do land on some distant shore, however, we find, on inspection, that it is our very home that we have suddenly rediscovered. But now we see it with new eyes, for while we were at home we were too close to it to see what it really was, to realize how much we loved it. We may have great enthusiasm for discovering something entirely new, but it brings nowhere near the delight of discovering what is already there.

Much of the delight of being a human being consists in our capacity to say of *what is,* "Now I see!" Most of what is really true is already known, even if we ourselves do not yet know it. This again brings me, in conclusion, to Belloc's idea of "discovery." Discovery means the way we go about finding answers to the important questions, to finding a real answer to a real question. Philosophy does not consist merely in asking questions. More importantly, it consists in finding answers to important questions as they are asked. "A process of reasoning which establishes the existence of a personal God is a *discovery,*" Belloc tells us. It is just as important that each of us discovers some basic philosophic truth as it is that we know the way around our own city.

Thus, it is important to know, to be aware, that we have minds. We need to recognize that the life of the mind is first contemplative, that is, it simply wants to know, to rejoice in *what is.* Thinking brings both joys and travails. That is, it is no fault of our being that we have to work, to discipline ourselves to know the important things, to ask the right questions, to recognize the right answers, to choose them when we know them. The intellectual life, the life of the mind, books, writing, conversing, yes, even walking and observing—these are things given to us.

I for one am fully convinced that on the day I die, there will be hundreds of books I will wish that I had read, many great thoughts left unwritten or unuttered, many a conversation with many a friend left unfinished, or perhaps not even begun. If Christ died at thirty-three, Socrates at seventy, and Plato at eighty-one, it is all right. We are not really deprived because none of them lived longer. For we meet our greatest teachers by reading what they have to tell us, even when, like Plato, they tell us that the very highest experiences cannot be written down.

We know that words lead us to things, to realities far too glorious ever to be completely captured by words alone. Books, as C. S. Lewis tells us, enable us to live many lives besides our own. This is their glory, and ours too. If we are relatively "illiterate" at forty, as Phyllis McGinley tells us, it may be a blessing, for only then are we really free to read what we once thought not worth reading. There are such things as "intellectual delights," and much of what is wrong with the world can be traced to the fact that many people, including ourselves, have not experienced these delights.

In the end, it is indeed a "risk" to be a human being. That risk consists largely in our choosing not to know *what is* because we do not want to know where such knowledge might lead us. I have often said that man is the "risk" of God because the only condition of man's initial existence was that he must be free to reject *what he is*. The other side of this same freedom, however, is that all things are given to us, even while we remain what we are. This is the real "discovery" and its "splendor." This is the life of the mind. Indeed, "it is possible," to recall Aquinas, "that in a single being, the comprehensiveness of the whole universe may dwell." At its best, human life, *the life of the mind*, consists of the splendor of this discovery. In asking the right questions, our minds may become open to all the answers that are *given* to it, to all the splendors of *what is*.

Three Appendices

To this relatively short book I have taken the liberty of adding three appendices. The reader may ignore them, but somehow I do not think the book would be complete without them. Yet I did not think they belonged in the central part of the text, the argument of which is otherwise complete. Let me briefly explain what they are.

The first appendix consists of a relatively brief list of books that, on being read, serve, I think, to nourish the life of any mind. They come from many angles and backgrounds. Each is a marvelous book; I suggest it because it is good. I like it when someone recommends to me a book to read, especially one about which I had previously known nothing. Naturally, I think others will like what I like.

The second appendix reproduces an interview on education and learning. And though this is not an "impersonal" book, this interview form allows me to say some things about my own background and enthusiasms that suggest how I understand this life of the mind we have sought to describe. This interview, in fact, was one of the reasons why I thought this book might be worth doing.

The third appendix was originally given as a sleepy summer afternoon lecture to some seminarians in Bridgeport, Connecticut. Msgr.

Kevin Royal, the rector of St. John Fischer Seminary, was rash enough to think that young men needed to hear something in praise of reading for mere pleasure, as well as for the broad cultivation of the mind. While this lecture is primarily directed at clerics, it is lightsome enough for anyone. The word "cleric" or "don" traditionally had both a secular and a religious meaning, referring to someone with formal academic or religious learning. The point of this reflection is not to present the technical books that a cleric—religious or lay—ought to read for his profession, but to recommend what he ought to read simply to be human, to be a gentleman in the sense that we discussed in the last chapter, by learning about those things which make us "gentle," those things which we love to know simply because they are delightful to know.

Appendix I

Schall's Twenty Books That Awaken the Mind

1. Josef Pieper, *Faith, Hope, and Love.*

2. C. S. Lewis, *An Experiment in Criticism.*

3. Leon Kass, *The Hungry Soul: Eating and the Perfection of Our Nature.*

4. Peter Kreeft, *The Philosophy of Tolkien.*

5. Dennis Quinn, *Iris Exiled: A Synoptic History of Wonder.*

6. Lorenzo Albacete, *God at the Ritz: Attraction to the Infinite.*

7. Frederick Wilhelmsen, *The Paradoxical Structure of Existence.*

8. Hilaire Belloc, *The Four Men.*

9. Robert Sokolowski, *The God of Faith and Reason.*

10. Jennifer Roback Morse, *Love and Economics: Why the Laissez-Faire Family Doesn't Work.*

11. Louis L'Amour, *The Education of a Wandering Man.*

12. G. K. Chesterton, *St. Thomas Aquinas*.

13. Robert Reilly, *Surprised by Beauty: A Listener's Guide to the Recovery of Modern Music*.

14. Tracey Rowland, *Culture and the Thomist Tradition*.

15. E. F. Schumacher, *A Guide for the Perplexed*.

16. Caryle Houselander, *Guilt*.

17. John Paul II, *Fides et Ratio*.

18. Ralph McInerny, *The Very Rich Hours of Jacques Maritain*.

19. Eric Voegelin, *Plato*.

20. Samuel Johnson, *Selected Essays*.

Plus one essay, Dorothy Sayers, "The Lost Tools of Learning," found easily on the Internet.

Appendix II

On Education and Knowledge

Responses to Questions Posed by Kathryn Jean Lopez,
National Review Online, 2002

1. "*How many years have you been teaching?*"
Before answering this question about years of teaching, I must first touch on the prior schooling question. As I like to put it, from the time I was five till I was thirty-seven, I only missed one academic year; the year I was in the Army, and even then I went to map-making school in the daytime and night school at Rutgers. To put this lengthy scholastic stint in context, once at my younger brother's home in California, a friend of his at a party asked me this very question about my years in school. My brother, who is not overly impressed with his clerical brother's weighty career, was listening to my response, which was "every year from five to thirty-seven." Before his friends could be too impressed, my brother quipped, "Yes, and if he had any brains, he would have graduated long ago."

I taught one year at the University of San Francisco (USF) in 1955–56—a course in logic, a political science course, and two courses in what was then called "Bone-Head English." The course of this wittily parodied name was designed to bolster those students who failed the standard English tests. We were to bring them up to par, as it were. I recall trying to teach them how to diagram a sentence. This effort, under my direction on the blackboard, made the classical Maze in Crete look positively simple.

From 1965 till 1969, I taught full time in the *Istituto Sociale* at the Gregorian University in Rome. From 1969 till 1977, I taught the spring semester in Rome and the fall semester at USF. Most people thought this an ideal arrangement. Its only drawback was that I was not at home in two places. From 1978 till the present, I have been teaching in the Government Department here at Georgetown. Sometimes, it is better to calculate teaching in terms of numbers of students rather than in numbers of years. I have averaged about two hundred and thirty students a year since 1979, give or take a few either way. After a few years, you realize that when a class walks out the door on the last day, the chances are very slim that you will ever see 95 percent of them again. It gives a certain poignancy to the art of teaching. Universities are not homes, but way stations, keepers of things no one else is likely to keep.

2. "*When did you know you wanted to teach?*"
Probably the best answer to this question about knowing when one wanted to teach is "after I thought I had something worth teaching." I have always thought that there was an intimate relation between teaching and writing. My priority has actually been writing, though my friend Father Robert Spitzer, S.J., now president of Gonzaga University, has argued that probably more people are reached through teaching. He has a point. While a student, I used to recommend to others that they take a class from a professor I knew was writing something, as this was probably, though not necessarily, a sign of aliveness. However, it is always possible for a very popular writer or teacher to be in fact a teacher of error, even a "good" teacher of error. No one should teach anything unless it is the truth, but, as my friend Professor Tom Martin at the University of Nebraska at Kearney recently wrote in *The Examined Life*,

academia today is generally ruled *ex professo* by Sophists who teach that there is no truth. Surveys show that this teaching is what the students understand to be the doctrine of most faculties. That is to say, they hold it is true that there is no truth, a contradiction as old as philosophy itself.

One should realize that the truth is free. Though it is addressed to every mind because it is a mind, no one "owns" it. While it is possible to "copyright" words or books, strictly speaking the truth belongs to everyone. It is a common experience for me, as I am sure it is for many, to read something that is really good. The first thing we want to do with reading something that moves us is to tell someone about it, almost anybody. Strictly speaking, we do not teach those who already know—our colleagues, for instance. We may argue with them, talk things over with them, but we do not teach them. Teaching implies a student's initial condition of not knowing and not knowing how to know. It refers to the passing from not knowing to knowing.

Yves Simon (in *A General Theory of Authority*) remarks that the role of a teacher is always substitutional. The end of teaching is when the teacher is not needed because the student sees the point himself. The teacher makes it easier for the student to pass from not knowing to knowing, generally because the teacher has been there before the student. But what is important is the end result when the non-knower knows, when the teacher disappears as no longer helpful. Essentially, the rule of parents is to make themselves unnecessary to the child, so that he can begin to rule himself. I like to tell students that I hope the day will come when they remember what they read in Aristotle, but forget that it was in Schall's class that they first encountered it. Aristotle is not "mine," even though it may be my way of insisting on him that caused or incited or forced someone to read him and, in reading him, to realize that he is great and speaks to them, even today, better than anyone else.

3. *"In your years of teaching, how have things changed in terms of the quality of the student, the quality of university life itself?"*
Often I am asked this question. My answer is that, as far as I can see, questions about the "quality" of the student or the "quality" of university life are relatively useless. The students I had in my first year here some twenty-five years ago were as good as and often better than students today. But the students I have today are also very good. Students today, in fact, have less leisure, less real time to be educated, most often because of "requirements." Often I think that if I were to put in a large pot all the students I ever had and drew each out one by one, I would not be able to tell what year each went to school and it would not make any difference.

The real issue is always what the student is required to read. And does he read it? My friend Professor Brian Benestad at the University of Scranton says, "Take them to the book." This is right. There is no university if Plato is not read, even if it is called a university. Students who go through a university never having read Plato or Aristotle or Augustine or Aquinas, among others, are really wasting most of their time and money. Without those thinkers, and also the Bible, they will not have a clue as to what it is all about.

And I am not necessarily an advocate of what are called "great books," not that I am against reading them, however defined. My *Another Sort of Learning*, in fact, was written because the great books are not adequate, even though they are "great." I agree with Leo Strauss and Frederick Wilhelmsen, both of whom remarked that the great books contradict each other. They can and often do lead to skepticism. Likewise, I agree with Plato in *The Republic* when he warns us of exposing students to great things too early, before they have lived long enough to recognize what is indeed great. I do not deny that some students are brighter than others. One of the functions of the university is to find out which is which. But I am also aware that learning is very often a question of whether someone has his soul in order, whether he can be attracted by *what is*. Great things will not be seen by those whose souls are not ordered. I did not say that first. Aristotle did. But I do not mind repeating it as if I were the first to discover it. Indeed, when we are taught something, when we finally see "the truth of things," to use Pieper's great expression, we do "discover" it. It is now we who see.

4. *"What makes a good teacher?"*
Some of the greatest teachers I have ever had would be called by most standards lousy teachers. One of the very finest teachers I ever had, Father Clifford Kossel, S.J., died about a week ago at Gonzaga University. If you did not sit in the front row and learn to lip-read, you would miss half of what he said, but what he said was terrific. In *Another Sort of Learning*, I recount the remark of René Latourelle, S.J., then dean at the Gregorian University, a French Canadian, and a good teacher and theologian. We were walking on the roof of the Gregorian University one night after supper when this question of what is a good teacher came up. Latourelle replied that this question will be answered in different ways according to when the question is asked—after the first day of class, after midterm, after finals, one year later, five years later, or thirty years later. Quite often, someone whom we thought was a bad teacher when we were young, turns out, when we are older, to have taught us more than anyone else.

Some say that good teachers are born not made. I have a cousin who was born on a farm in Iowa, as was I. He is my age (ancient), never went to college, and he worked on a farm or in the defense industry all his life. He had what Aristotle would call a practical intellect when it came to making or organizing things. I do not ever recall being in an uninteresting conversation with him. On the other hand, many years of working over a subject matter no doubt makes us better able to understand and teach something. There is a kind of "antiwisdom" in academia today. Young professors are concerned with new things. And there is nothing more exhilarating than a young man or woman just out of graduate school, someone who has really learned something. I just read a doctoral thesis on Strauss from the University of Adelaide in

Australia that was positively thrilling. But there are some things that require years of going over again and again.

I like to cite C. S. Lewis's remark that "[i]f you have only read a great book once, you have not read it at all." My addendum to that remark is that every time you read, say, Aristotle's *Ethics,* even after you have read it fifty or sixty times, you will find something startlingly new in it, something that you never saw before. This morning, for example, I was reading the second book of the *Ethics.* I came across the following passage, which I had indeed underlined semesters ago. I saw that this passage had previously struck me: "For, first, we do not decide to do what is impossible, and anyone claiming to decide to do it would seem a fool; but we do wish for what is impossible, e.g. never to die, as well as for what is possible" (1111b21–22). When read attentively, the whole structure of reason and revelation, a topic on which I have often written, is contained in this one brief passage.

So what "makes" a good teacher? Basically, a good teacher is someone who leads us to ask the important questions, without at the same time being someone who suggests that there are no answers to such questions. The real mystery of teaching is not that there are questions, but that there are answers. Nor would I deny the paradoxical fact that students also "teach" teachers. A good teacher knows that out there in the classroom there is always likely to be someone brighter than he is. Michael P. Jackson is a former deputy secretary of transportation in the Bush administration. He was a student here about twenty years ago. I learned much from him. What students do is to enable their professors to reflect again and again on the materials that the students usually see only once, while they are young.

5. "*Are there any great teachers among us in public life today?*"
The purpose of "public life" is not to teach, but to make good laws and to give good examples of how to live well. Teaching is first a very private thing that belongs to the contemplative order, to things for their own sakes. This is even true of teaching the crafts and arts of human action,

even though these latter in their truth are ordained to doing or making. Laws, as Aristotle and Aquinas maintain, can be educative—should be, in fact. We can indeed be corrupted by the example of public men. This is in part what the lesson of the Clinton administration was about. But public men are not strictly speaking teachers. This is not to deny that the worst form of corruption ultimately comes not from politicians but from errant philosophers, as St. Paul and Plato understood. The great drama of the *Gorgias* of Plato centers on the dangerous public man rejecting the philosopher by refusing to engage him in conversation. The public man can and often does refuse to examine his conscience and his premises.

But Machiavelli understood that the real way to change a society is to change the souls of the potential philosophers, to write a book, not to rule. Plato knew this too. Plato knew it first. This is why Machiavelli tried so hard to remove the examples and teachings of Socrates and Christ, men who never wrote books, from the souls of potential philosophers and rulers.

The greatest teacher in public life today, the one who has talked to more human beings than any other man in history, is, no doubt, John Paul II. But he stands in a post beyond public life. He tells the young all over the world that the first thing they need to attend to is their own souls. Not a few worry that the pope does not discipline or govern as well as he teaches and encourages. But this goes back to the fact that it is one thing to teach and another thing to rule, though the latter without the former, the public life without the truth, can corrupt us all by its example if we do not already have counteracting worthy habits.

6. *"What is the most educational book ever written?"*
No other book can match *The Republic* of Plato, or, *a pari,* all of the works of Plato. I touched on this in my essay, "The Death of Plato," in the *American Scholar* (Summer 1996). The best modern teacher is Josef Pieper, though C. S. Lewis, by comparison, is not second. What about Aristotle and Aquinas? What about Augustine? Aquinas was very deliberate at making things clear so that beginners could quickly and

easily get to the highest things. Peter Kreeft is very good in representing Aquinas, and Lewis, and Pascal, and Job, and Tolkien. One cannot oppose Plato, Aristotle, Augustine, and Aquinas to each other. The later figures always presuppose the former and add something. I have just finished rereading the Tolkien trilogy. Everything is there, too, in its own way. And Strauss and Voegelin loom large in the horizon of our own time.

7. *"Is there any advice you would give to young teachers starting out, who are possibly discouraged by the liberalism among the faculty and lack of enthusiasm among the students?"*
One thing to do is read the *American Enterprise* magazine on diversity in the colleges (July 2002, I think). Basically, there is little if any political diversity in college faculties or administrations. All promotions, all rank and tenure are decided by the same narrow political criteria. For the most part it means that no one can really get an education in most colleges. Education must be pursued independently, which is the good side of individualism. One has to find journals and fora wherein one can speak or write. One has to learn to speak the truth without glory. It is not easy. My advice is that found in Aristotle, "This sort of inquiry is, to be sure, unwelcome to us, when those who introduced the Forms [Plato] were friends of ours; still, it presumably seems better, indeed only right, to destroy even what is close to us if that is the way to preserve the truth. And we must especially do this when we are philosophers, lovers of wisdom; for though we love both the truth and our friends, piety requires us to honor the truth more" (1096a14–17). This is an agenda for a very humble life. But it also reminds us to seek the "pearl of great price." Nothing else will really satisfy us.

8. *"As you are constantly citing both, what message do Plato and Charlie Brown have in common?"*
Both Plato and Charlie Brown are charming. Plato in part wrote *The Republic* to "out-charm" Homer. Charles Schulz wrote *Peanuts* to cause

generations to think of Christian theology without knowing what they were doing. Read Robert Short's *The Gospel According to Peanuts* or *The Parables of Peanuts* or Charles Schulz's *The Beagles and the Bunnies Shall Lie Down Together: The Theology in Peanuts*. I swear I have cited every incident in this last book in some political or theological context. Charlie Brown is a good man for whom something always goes wrong. Plato knows that things go wrong. His whole life is devoted to founding a republic in speech in which things go right. To put this city in speech in our souls is the essence of what it is to know.

But of course, Schulz wants us to know that Lucy will never allow Charlie to kick the ball without her pulling it away at the last minute. Behind Charlie and behind Plato, there lurks a tremendous joy. Chesterton also pointed this out at the end of *Orthodoxy*. Plato called us the "playthings of the gods," that is to say, we exist but we need not. We do not exist because it is necessary that we exist. Therefore, if we exist, it is because we are, but need not be. Yet our existence is worthy. Plato remarks that something was lacking to creation after it was all put out there. What was lacking was someone to praise it.

Charlie Brown—the parallel text, in a way, is Chesterton's book, *St. Thomas Aquinas*—exists to praise and remember even the oddest things, his watching TV while his sister Sally wants him to help her with her homework. It is often said that Plato forms the abstract from the particular. Somehow they needed to be subsumed into the Word made flesh so that nothing small would ever again be unimportant, even if it did not need to exist. If we spend our days reading Plato and Charlie Brown, we will soon arrive at *what is*, which is where we want to be in any case. There are other ways to arrive at the same place. But this way is the most pleasant and charming.

Appendix III

READING FOR CLERICS

Father Latour arranged an order for his last days; if routine was necessary to him in health, it was even more so in sickness. . . . Morning prayers over, Magdalena came with his breakfast, and he sat in his easy chair while she made his bed and arranged his room. Then he was ready to see visitors. The Archbishop came in for a few moments, when he was at home; the Mother Superior, the American doctor. Bernard read aloud to him the rest of the morning; St. Augustine, or the letters of Madame de Sévigné, or his favorite Pascal.
> —Willa Cather, *Death Comes for the Archbishop*

Every author has a meaning in which all the contradictory passages agree, or he has no meaning at all. We cannot affirm the latter of Scripture and the prophets; they undoubtedly are full of good sense. We must then seek for a meaning which reconciles all discrepancies.
> —Pascal, *Pensées*

The Life of the Mind

I

A friend of mine in Florida, the columnist Mary Jo Anderson, once wrote to me that "God had taken her off of the tennis courts." When I inquired just why it was "God" who ended her tennis career, she replied:

> The short-ish version is that I had piled up quite a stack of Catholic books on the bedside table to read. I promised God I'd get to them when my last child went to college. And when he departed, I picked up a tennis racquet instead and within two years, I was playing tennis four times a week. . . . Then, when I passed the stack of books one day, I said to myself, "Lord, some day when I get time." I went downstairs, and rolled up a rug to take to be cleaned. It was too heavy—result, bulging disc. The orthopedic surgeon tried several remedies. . . . None worked. He put me to bed for three months. I had plenty of time to read. I tried to resume playing; finally I got the message. I put the racquet away and turned my attention elsewhere.

As a result of putting the tennis racquet away, she began to read.

Mrs. Anderson was a college graduate who, like many of us, did not read much in college, or much of what was worth reading. "Why didn't anyone tell me about these books?" she once asked me. But we have to be ready to listen when we are told about them. She has, in fact, as those who read her know, become a good, careful reader, not just of Catholic books, but of others, too. Her implied conclusion is that if we do not voluntarily keep our promises to God to read, He will see to their fulfillment some other, less pleasant, way. God thinks reading important!

This lesson about reading is not to take anything away from tennis or golf or the value and need of relaxation or exercise in one's life. Indeed, I think that the lessons we learn from sports, both from playing and watching them, have manifest and even profound lessons for both the life of the mind and the life of faith. But the lesson is that if we want to make time for what is worthwhile, we have to look at our priorities and see these in the light of a real hierarchy.

In this reflection, I am not going to advocate reading on the grounds of "obligation," though I think that is an element of any argument for why we ought to read, just as practicing wind-sprints are an element in winning races. We can say, for example, that we are "obliged" to read the Epistle to the Romans because we are clerics, because that is our profession. It may take some further prodding, however, to "make" us read it along with the other books we may need to help us understand it—commentaries or dictionaries, for instance.

Another friend of mine, Anne Burleigh, the author of a very insightful book called *Journey Up the River*, wrote to me about her grandson: "He has taken off like a shot with his reading. He has just finished first grade and just read D'Aulaire's *Book of Greek Myths*. He is halfway through *Treasure Island*. What a great thing to learn to read. There is no joy quite like it." It is something of this spirit that I want to suffuse these remarks for us clerics, though we are well beyond first grade. I prefer to emphasize the spirit of Father Latour. You will notice what he had read to him, even as he was dying—St. Augustine, Madame de Sévigné, and Pascal, "his favorite." These are the books of a priest who knows about reading.

I recount these earlier reflections of my friends because I suspect that its lesson is one that many a cleric has had to learn, or wishes he had learned, in his lifetime.

II

John Paul II once told some Indian bishops:

Proper theological preparation requires instruction which, while respecting that part of the truth found in other religions, nevertheless unfailingly proclaims that Jesus Christ is the Way and

the Truth and the Life. To this end Catholic educational institutions must offer a sound philosophical formation which is
necessary for the study of theology. Truth transcends the limi-
tations of both Eastern and Western thought and unites every
culture and society. (June 27, 2003)

I take this admonition as a charter to priests to keep their intellectual
interests, including those having to do with theology, broad and in-
formed.

Catholicism, for better or worse, is a religion of intelligence. That
is, it has always recognized, as Leo Strauss pointed out, that philosophy
is essential to its overall understanding and mission. *Fides et Ratio*, John
Paul's encyclical on reason and revelation, is quite clear, even blunt, on
the need and practice of genuine philosophy. In this light, I was rather
disappointed that the recent lengthy *Instruction from the Congregation
for the Clergy*, "The Priest, Pastor and Leader of the Parish Community" (*L'Osservatore Romano,* January 15, 2005), did not contain some
specific mention of this aspect of the priestly life.

The *Instruction* did mention, however, the Divine Office. "In the
Divine Office he [the priest] supplies what is lacking in the praise of
Christ and, as an accredited ambassador, his intercession for the salvation of the world is numbered among the most effective" (#14). But
while the Office is an act of praise, it is also an act of or exercise in
intelligence. There is no daily Office that does not contain some basic
and profound insight into the nature of things, divine and human.
The second readings are often gems of reflective profundity from the
Greek fathers, Augustine, Teresa of Avila, the great popes, a Gregory,
or a Leo. There is a relation between worship and intelligence that is
brought home to us every day in the Office. Moreover, the repetition
of these basic readings year after year—even, in some instances, daily,
weekly, or monthly—gives us a lesson in reading that recalls C. S.
Lewis's quip that if you have only read a great book once, you have not
read it at all.

It is my general observation, however, that the work of any good priest in almost any parish in the world, if he is doing even half of what he should be doing, takes more time and energy than he has or ever could hope to have. Prudence means doing what we can and living with it. God does not ask us to be supermen, even when our bishops or superiors seem to disagree. I still recall having celebrated Sunday Mass in the parish of one of my nephews on a visit in Texas. The pastor was there after Mass. I asked him how many parishioners he had. "Twenty-three thousand," he told me. I was astounded. "Do you have any help?" "Yes, I have two assistants plus a Jesuit who comes in on Sundays." In other words, the man's normal life was simply to be overwhelmed, with or without the Jesuit.

Good bishops and religious superiors often have to chide, cajole, or even command that time be given, not just to prayer and spiritual life, but also to the life of the intellect. Yet, in the Church of Rome, an intelligent priesthood is not a luxury. The newspapers, alas, are full of what happens when we do not have a virtuous priesthood. The relation between mind and virtue is not of minimal importance. Most failures of intellect, I suspect, can be traced back to a prior failure of virtue, of spiritual life. Still, there are, I think, few more fatal mistakes for a cleric than that of underestimating the importance of his own intellectual life. I mean by this that he must have some intelligent grasp of why Catholicism is true, and some awareness of the arguments and practices that purport to deny this truth.

III

Where does one get the time to nurture one's intellectual life? The first step today, I suppose, is to examine how much time we give to television, the Internet, and other such absorbing modern technologies. I acknowledge that in a very restricted sense, when we control them and not they us, they can be useful. But one must make a general declaration of independence from them. We can only do that if we have a source of information and knowledge that is independent of their influence. This is one of the things we need to put in place. I do not just mean that the media are sometimes wrong or subtly ideological. If our only source of news is PBS or the local newspaper or television station, we are probably in serious trouble. We have need of a few intelligent or scholarly journals or websites that provide genuine alternatives to the content of the media. It is never neutral, as my friend Tracey Rowland has shown in her new book, *Culture and the Thomist Tradition*.

An army officer friend of mine recommended to my attention a book on the Marine Corps called *Absolutely Americans*. He remarked that the book portrays well both the nobility and the disorder of troops. Young soldiers are often addicted to Internet pornography. And "addicted" is probably the right word. No doubt we need to be aware that pastoral guidance today has to include the disorders of the soul and mind that can come, if we let them, from the Internet or other such sources.

We all know that the Internet also contains, on any given day, all the news from the Vatican, many good Catholic websites, the *New Catholic Encyclopedia*, the works of St. Thomas Aquinas or almost any saint. It can be and is a most useful tool. But it can also be corrupting. We are not going to get much help in controlling this allure from outside of ourselves. The government has become itself an active player in this corruption in many ways. Virtue has always been a matter, largely, of self-discipline. This is doubly so today.

What is the alternative? I suggest that in today's world, the only alternative is to pursue truth seriously and steadily all of our lives. I conceive this primarily as a joy. One of the first books I would recommend to learn how to have the time to read what we want to read is the western writer Louis L'Amour's *The Education of a Wandering Man*. This book was given to me by a friend long after I was approaching senility, so much of its advice I had already learned from my own mistakes and experiences. I have written my own guides to reading in *Another Sort of Learning* and *On the Unseriousness of Human Affairs*.

But I have often recommended L'Amour to others. Its advice about how to find time to read, how to record and remember what we read, indeed how to go about systematically learning about something—say, the Smith and Wesson pistol, or the gullies in Wyoming—is both graphic and useful. Aside, perhaps, from A. D. Sertillanges' classic, *The Intellectual Life*, no book is quite so helpful as L'Amour's in helping us learn how to organize our time and how to learn what we do not know, even what we do not want or need to know.

IV

As I have suggested, Catholicism is a religion of intelligence. It is likewise a religion of revelation, but it conceives this revelation as coming from and directed to intelligence, that is, as directed to the truth of things. We are fortunate if our seminary education gave us some adequate literary, historical, and philosophical background. We are usually relatively young when we are ordained, at least by Greek standards. We cannot be just "theologians" and still be theologians. Yet we need not consider ourselves to be universal geniuses either. We will always meet people more intelligent, better educated than ourselves. This is something in which we can rejoice, without forgetting that not a few of the most brilliant people who have ever lived have been priests—including Aquinas, Augustine, Newman, Francis de Sales, and Bernard of Clairvaux. I think we are wise to keep at our fingertips the reflections of priests who are also notable intellectuals—Romano Guardini, for example, or Henri de Lubac, or Hans Urs von Balthasar, or Josef Ratzinger. I would place Karol Wojtyla also in this category.

A priest needs to have and to cultivate his own library. I recently had the pleasure of staying at the parish of Msgr. Stephen di Giovanni in downtown Stamford, Connecticut. He is a scholar in his own right, having written a very excellent study of how the *New York Times* reported the relation of Pius XII and the Jews all during and immediately following World War II. Very favorably, it turns out. His study, I was not surprised to see, contains a marvelous collection of books. I am only sorry I did not think to copy down the titles of some of them.

Looking through my own shelves, I found a book I had almost forgotten, the anthology George Schuster, the former president of Hunter College, once compiled titled *The World's Great Catholic Literature*. If you see a used book with such a title, it is probably worth having. One of the brief selections in this book was Giovanni Boccaccio's observations on Dante. For our purposes, it is worth citing. Not knowing something of Dante, after all, is to miss half the grandeur and delight of Catholicism. "In his studies, he [Dante] was most assiduous," Boccaccio tells us, "insomuch that while he was occupied therewith no news that he heard could divert him from them." To prove this point, Boccaccio charmingly tells us that once in Siena, in front of an apothecary shop, someone presented Dante with a little book that he had not before seen. It was unnamed but, to quote Boccaccio, "very famous among the men of understanding." Who could resist that description?

Dante was so excited to read this book that he immediately stretched himself out on his stomach on a bench in front of the shop. He began to read. Meanwhile, all around him was going on a big sporting event, with bands, dancing girls, yells and screams, sort of the Sienese version of the Super Bowl. But, unperturbed, Dante read on for three straight hours, from three to six in the afternoon. "Yet he afterwards declared to some who asked him how he could keep from watching so fine a festival as had taken place before him that he had heard nothing. Whereupon," Boccaccio adds, "to the first wonder of the questioners was not unduly added a second."[1]

Now, I do not necessarily intend to commend here always stretching out on the floor during the Rose Bowl to read a book "very famous among the men of understanding." But I do not intend to knock the practice either. I usually spend Christmas vacation with my brother and family in San Diego. We rarely miss the big games on New Year's Day. But I do vividly recall reading Dostoevsky's *The Possessed* during

Christmas vacation, even though it interfered some with the football watching. Of course, I might add, *The Possessed* is a book "very famous among the men of understanding," as is all of Dostoevsky. He is an author whose treatment of the priesthood itself and of the human condition generally is something no priest should miss.

V

Another reason we priests should be readers, readers of what is most profound among us, is that, however large our experience of human nature, and a priest's exposure is usually greater than most, it is never large enough for what we need to know about our flock or even ourselves. Plato was very aware of this need and of its dangers. C. S. Lewis put it well:

> Those of us who have been true readers all our lives seldom fully realize the enormous extension of our being which we owe to authors. We realize it best when we talk with an unliterary friend. He may be full of goodness and good sense but he inhabits a tiny world. In it we should be suffocated. The man who is content to be only himself, and therefore less a self, is in prison. My own eyes are not enough for me. . . . Literary experience heals the wound, without undermining the privilege, of individuality. . . . But in reading great literature I become a thousand men and yet remain myself. Like the night sky in the Greek poem, I see with a myriad eyes, but it is still I who see. Here, as in worship, in love, in moral action, and in knowing, I transcend myself; and am never more myself than when I do.[2]

It would be difficult to find a more insightful passage.

This C. S. Lewis book, incidentally, *An Experiment in Criticism*, was first published in 1961. I never heard of it until a former student gave it to me for my seventy-fifth birthday. The book astounded me. The point is that it is never too late. As my friend in Florida exclaimed, "Why did not someone tell me about these books?" We cannot always blame someone else. I might suggest too, that most of us have sisters or brothers or parents or cousins who give us Christmas and birthday presents. We get shirts and sweaters. I suggest that having a goodly list of books we would like to read handy when we are asked what we want for Christmas is a good idea, not that we don't need and appreciate the sweaters also.

VI

Probably, the greatest book ever written explaining why bishops should not be married is Anthony Trollope's famous novel *Barchester Towers*. It is not to be missed, especially if one wants to be a bishop. However, we find here also, by way of irony, just why our clergy should be liberally educated and keep their awareness of what the world is like. "There is, perhaps, no greater hardship at present inflicted on mankind in civilized and free countries than the necessity of listening to sermons. . . . With what complacency will a young parson deduce false conclusions from misunderstood texts, and then threaten us with all the penalties of Hades if we neglect to comply with the instructions he gives us!"[3] We would be deaf today, many of us, if we did not frequently hear similar criticisms of our sermons.

In Western literature, the sermon is also an art form. We have but to read Newman to realize this, if we have not already. Newman's name alone should be enough to remind us of our essential need to be men of mind and intelligence. I would not deny that the Curé of Ars or the Country Priest in the Bernanos novel were simple, even rather unlearned men. But they were holy and wise men, mostly exempt from the vanity or pride that is often associated with the more learned.

VII

There exists a volume titled *The World of Wodehouse Clergy.* My own copy was another gift from friends. It too was a book I had never heard of before it was given to me. It is one of the most amusing books I know. It does not lack that quality of a good novel, even a humorous novel, of enabling us to see ourselves. Again, like the clerics in Trollope, the family of the Mulliners in Wodehouse are members of the clerical orders in the Church of England. No doubt this is a book full of insight and amusement about the human condition, the unique humor of which seems to be made especially possible by the very existence of Christianity.

In one memorable scene, the bishop of Stortford, who I believe is a Mulliner, comes down into his living room where his daughter, Kathleen, of whom he is naturally protective, is sitting reading what the bishop at first thought was "a book of devotion." In fact, it was a novel titled *Cocktail Time*—a title perhaps intentionally redolent of T. S. Eliot's *Cocktail Party.* Trying to be unobtrusive, the bishop stealthily read, over his daughter's shoulder, some passages from the middle of chapter 13. Alarmed by what he read, the bishop-parent grabbed the book from the girl. He returned it to his study to see "if he had really seen what he thought he had." As Wodehouse puts it, "He had."

The bishop's church was called, delicately, "St. Jude the Resilient, Eaton Square." The following Sunday, in the pulpit himself, the bishop spoke on the text of Ecclesiasticus 13:1, "He that touches pitch shall be defiled." The core of the sermon was an attack on a novel called *Cocktail Time.* To an undoubtedly startled congregation, "he described it as obscene, immoral, shocking, impure, corrupt, shameless, graceless and depraved." Now, what do we suppose was the effect of this astonishing sermon of the bishop of Stortford in the pulpit of St. Jude the Resilient? Here is Wodehouse's description: "All over the sacred edifice you could see eager men jotting the name (of the novel) down on their cuffs, scarcely able to wait to add it to their library list."[4] Here, in a brief passage, we have insight into the dangers of a naïve clergy, into why censorship usually does not work, into the power of novels, into male human nature, and, finally, into how to build up our libraries, though not, to be sure, necessarily ones with the most edifying books.

VIII

In 1926, G. K. Chesterton wrote an essay titled "Why I Am a Catholic." What I have been attempting to do in these remarks about clerical reading is to remind us that we are, in a way, in a very privileged position. Everyday, just in reading our Breviary, we come across ideas, persons, and insights from almost every century and from a wide variety of people. What the Venerable Bede said is not alien to us. Both the Council of Nicea and the First Vatican Council dealt with things that remain pertinent to us and, when we reread them, refresh us. The Psalms are with us daily, as is some text from the New Testament, the epistles, and the Old Testament. In a large class, few will know who the Good Samaritan was, let alone what the Acts of the Apostles were, or who Albert the Great was. But we know these things.

Chesterton saw that things fit together. If a thing was past, it did not mean that it was unimportant or that it was not present within our own world, only that we did not recognize it. "Nine out of ten of what we call new ideas," Chesterton wrote,

> are simply old mistakes. The Catholic Church has for one of her chief duties that of preventing people from making those old mistakes; from making them over and over again forever, as people always do if they are left to themselves. The Catholic Church carries a sort of map of the mind which looks like the map of a maze, but which is in fact a guide to the maze. It has been compiled from knowledge which, even considered as a human knowledge, is quite without any human parallel. There is no other case of one continuous intelligent institution that has been thinking about thinking for two thousand years.[5]

Our reading, to use Chesterton's notion, keeps our maps of intellectual reality from being merely an intellectual maze.

Basically, I want to say that a priest should first of all manifest himself as someone who loves the truth, even in a world that maintains that it is true that there is no truth. This love of truth is not just an intellectual quest, but it is at least that. No priest can afford to lack some of that fierce determination to become a philosopher, to know the truth that Augustine manifested in his *Confessions*. And while I do not conceive that the pursuit of truth is only or primarily a matter of books or formal learning—wisdom resides too in the unlearned, as surely we all know from the experience of those who are wise—I do insist that an intrinsic component of Catholicism is precisely books and formal learning. Perhaps I should rather say that it is the active mind that seeks the knowledge of what is with the help of books.

IX

If I were to recommend one book or author that every priest should read immediately and regularly, it would not be the book of a priest, but rather *Josef Pieper: An Anthology*.[6] I recommend this particular book by way of suggesting that reading the whole corpus of Pieper, most of which is reflected in this *Anthology*, is a fundamental way to keep intellectually alert and aware of the depths of both reason and revelation. It is also the best introduction to St. Thomas Aquinas and a constant reminder of how important Aquinas is to us. Pieper himself is the clearest and briefest of all the philosophers. He is a marvel of lucidity and historical context. He does not neglect the poets, nor should we. Above all, he seeks the truth and is a sure guide for those who know enough about themselves to see that this is what we should be about.

But I do not necessarily want in this reflection on reading for clerics to concentrate only on books that are Catholic. Aristotle and Plato are at the top of any list. Chesterton tells us in *Orthodoxy* that he became a Catholic *because*, as it were, he never read a Catholic book. He had only read the heretics and read them carefully. If we are taught any lesson from John Paul II, it is that we should accept truth wherever we find it. On the other hand, this does not deny that we are more likely to find it in some places than others. In his very wise book, *Iris Exiled: A Synoptic History of Wonder,* Dennis Quinn has written, "With the advent of Christ, it became clear how and why we must love our neighbor—not for their own sakes but because of and for the love of God. Wonder then turned wholly toward the absolute mystery beyond self and society, and, insofar as it was under biblical inspiration, the focus of wonder shifted decisively from the subject wondering to the object wondered at and to the relationship between the two."[7] "Wonder," of course, is the great Aristotelian word that defines best why it is that we freely seek to know *what is* and its causes.

A priest, I think, should above all be someone who is drawn to where he is, to what he holds and to how he lives because he is seen to be freely pursuing where reality leads him. Wise reading will be what enables us not only to avoid recommending *Cocktail Time* to our congregations when we become bishops, but to become the thousand men who have seen the "the truth of things." We need not perhaps always read with the avidity of a Dante, but let it be said of us that we have allied ourselves with those who have been "thinking about thinking for two thousand years." At our end, let us also remember what Father Latour had read to him in his last days—Augustine, the letters of Madame de Sévigné, and Pascal, "his favorite."

Notes

Introduction

1. Hannah Arendt, *The Life of the Mind* (New York: Harcourt Brace and Jovanovich, 1978), Vol. I, "Thinking," Vol. II. "Willing." Reviewed in *Theological Studies* 40 (March 1979), 204–6.
2. Ibid., Vol. I, 59.
3. Walker Percy, *Lost in the Cosmos: The Last Self-Help Book* (New York: Farrar, Strauss, & Giroux, 1983).

Chapter I

1. The two books that most parallel this Sertillanges book, both in terms of difficulty and in terms of content, are Mortimer Adler's *How to Read a Book* and Peter Redpath's *How to Read a Difficult Book*.

Chapter II

1. C. S. Lewis, *An Experiment in Criticism* (Cambridge: Cambridge University Press, [1964] 2002), 2.
2. Ibid., 48.
3. The essay is in *On the Unseriousness of Human Affairs* (Wilmington, DE: ISI Books, 2002), 63–82.

Chapter III

1. See G. K. Chesterton, "On the Classics," in *Come to Think of It* (New York: Dodd, Mead, 1931), 53–58.

2. Leo Strauss, "Jerusalem and Athens: Some Preliminary Reflections," in *Studies in Platonic Political Philosophy*, ed. Thomas Pangle (Chicago: University of Chicago Press, 1983), 147–73.

3. See James V. Schall, "The Keenest of Intellectual Pleasures," *Gilbert!* 4 (March 2001), 18–19.

4. See Étienne Gilson, *Reason and Revelation in the Middle Ages* (New York: Scribner's, 1938).

5. Josef Pieper, *Leisure: The Basis of Culture*, trans. G. Malsbary (South Bend, IN: St. Augustine's Press, 1998).

6. See Frederick Wilhelmsen, "Great Books: Enemies of Wisdom?" *Modern Age* 31 (Summer/Fall 1987), 323–31.

7. Mortimer Adler, "What Is Liberal Education?" http//www.realuofe.org/libed/adler/wle.html.

8. See "The Seven Liberal Arts," http://www.cosmopolis.com/villa/liberal-arts.html.

9. Evelyn Waugh, *Brideshead Revisited* (Boston: Little, Brown, 1945), 9.

10. Yves Simon, "Freedom from the Self," *A General Theory of Authority* (Notre Dame, IN: University of Notre Dame Press, 1980), 151–52. The reference from St. Thomas is to *De Veritate*, 2.2.

11. See on this point E. F. Schumacher's *A Guide for the Perplexed* (New York: Harper Colophon, 1977).

12. Donald Kagan, "What Is a Liberal Education?" The McDermott Papers (Irving, TX: University of Dallas, 2001).

13. See, for a still masterly treatment of this topic, Joseph Lins, "The Seven Liberal Arts," *The Catholic Encyclopedia* (New York: Appleton, 1912), Vol. I, 760–65.

14. See Leo Strauss, "What Is Liberal Education?" *Liberalism: Ancient and Modern* (Chicago: University of Chicago Press, 1968), 3–8.

15. See Schall, *Another Sort of Learning* (San Francisco: Ignatius Press, 1988); *A Student's Guide to Liberal Learning* (Wilmington, DE: ISI Books, 1997).

16. Jacques Maritain, "Education and the Humanities," in *The Education of Man: The Educational Philosophy of Jacques Maritain*, ed. Donald and Idella Gallagher (Garden City, NJ: Doubleday, 1962), 85.
17. Cicero, *Selected Works*, ed. Michael Grant (Harmondsworth, UK: Penguin, 1960), 159.
18. *Boswell's Life of Johnson* (London: Oxford, 1931), II, 3.
19. John Henry Newman, *The Idea of a University* (Garden City, NJ: Doubleday, 1959), 144.
20. Ibid., 145.
21. See Herbert Deane, *The Political and Social Ideas of St. Augustine* (New York: Columbia University Press, 1956).
22. "Man is not properly speaking human but superhuman." St. Thomas, *De Virtutibus Cardinalibus*, I.

Chapter IV

1. Mel Lazarus, *Miss Peach, Again* (New York: Grosset, 1972).
2. Gilbert Highet, *Poets in a Landscape* (London: Hamish Hamilton, 1957), 198.
3. *Boswell's Life of Johnson* (London: Oxford, 1931), Vol. I, 131.
4. Ibid., I, 132.
5. Wendell Berry, *A Place on Earth: Revision* (New York: Farrar, 1983), 176.
6. J. R. R. Tolkien, *The Hobbit* (New York: Ballantine, 1970), 16.
7. J. R. R. Tolkien, *The Return of the King* (New York: Ace, n.d.), 248.
8. Anton Myrer, *Once an Eagle* (New York: Berkeley Medallion, 1968), 244.
9. P. G. Wodehouse, *How Right You Are, Jeeves* (New York: Avon, 1976), 115.

Chapter V

1. See James V. Schall, "The Death of Plato," *American Scholar* 65 (Summer 1996), 401–15.
2. Sheed, "Milk for Babes," in *Sidelights on the Catholic Revival*, 66.
3. Margaret Craven, *Again Calls the Owl* (New York: Laurel, 1980), 37.

Chapter VI

1. Charles N. R. McCoy, *The Structure of Political Thought* (New York: McGraw-Hill, 1963), 77–98.

2. Leo Strauss, *The City and Man* (Chicago: University of Chicago Press, 1964), 241.

3. *Boswell's Life of Johnson* (New York: Oxford, 1931), II, 26.

4. Charles Schulz, *Here Comes Charlie Brown* (New York: Fawcett, 1957).

5. David Schindler, *Heart of the World, Center of the Church* (Grand Rapids, MI: Eerdmans, 1996), 205.

6. Robert Sokolowski, *Eucharistic Presence: A Study of the Theology of Disclosure* (Washington: Catholic University of America Press, 1994), 14.

Chapter VII

1. Belloc, "On Old Towns," in *Selected Essays of Hilaire Belloc* (London: Methuen, 1941), 277.

2. Jean-Jacques Rousseau, *The Reveries of the Solitary Walker*, trans. C. Butterworth (New York: Harper Colophon, 1979), 12.

3. Belloc, "Arles," in *Hills and the Sea*, (Marlboro: The Marlboro Press, 1906), 61.

4. Belloc, preface to Vincent McNabb, *The Catholic Church and Philosophy* (New York: Macmillan, 1927).

5. Belloc, "On Sailing the Seas," in *Selected Essays of Hilaire Belloc*, 143.

6. Ibid., 148.

7. Belloc, "The Harbour of the North," in *Hills and the Sea*, 216.

8. Ibid., 217.

9. Ibid., 218–19.

10. Ibid., 220.

11. Belloc, "Treves," *Selected Essays*, ed. J. B. Morton (Harmondsworth, UK: Penguin, 1958), 189–90.

12. Ibid., 190–91.

13. Ibid., 191.

14. Belloc, "René Descartes," in *Characters of the Reformation* (Garden City, NJ: Doubleday Image, 1961), 172.

15. Ibid., 174.

16. Ibid.

17. Ibid., 176.
18. Ibid.
19. Belloc, "Blaise Pascal," in *Charaters of the Reformation*, 178.
20. Ibid., 181.
21. Ibid., 182.
22. Ibid., 183.
23. Belloc, "Lynn," in *Hills and the Sea*, 100.
24. Ibid., 100–101.
25. Ibid., 104.

Chapter VIII

1. *The Letters of J. R. R. Tolkien,* ed. H. Carpenter (Boston: Houghton Mifflin, 1981), 98.
2. Plutarch, *The Lives of the Noble Grecians and Romans,* trans. J. Dryden, revised by Arthur Hugh Clough (New York: Modern Library, n. d.), 918.
3. Schulz, *"Could You Be More Pacific?"* (New York: Topper Books, 1988).
4. *The Education of Henry Adams: An Autobiography* (New York: Time, 1964), 62.
5. Ibid., 59.
6. Samuel L. Clemens, *Life on the Mississippi* (New York: Lancer, 1968), 459–62.

Chapter IX

1. Pieper, "The Truth of All Things," in *Living the Truth* (San Francisco: Ignatius Press, 1989).
2. Allan Bloom, *The Closing of the American Mind* (New York: Simon & Schuster, 1986), 25.
3. Eric Voegelin, *Conversations with Eric Voegelin*, ed. R. Eric O'Connor (Montreal: Thomas More Papers 176, 1980).
4. Pieper, "The Sacred and 'Desacralization,'" in *Problems of Modern Faith*, trans. J. Van Heurck (Chicago: Franciscan Herald Press, 1974), 39.
5. Belloc, *The Path to Rome*, 102.
6. Frederick Nietzsche, *Beyond Good and Evil: Towards a Philosophy of the Future* (Harmondsworth, UK: Penguin, 1976).

7. James Thurber, *My Life and Hard Times* (New York: Bantam, 1968), 13.
8. Charles Schulz, *Here Comes Charlie Brown* (New York: Fawcett, 1957).

Chapter X
1. Pieper, *Enthusiasm and the Divine Madness: On the Platonic Dialogue, Phaedrus*, trans. R. and C. Winston (New York: Harcourt, 1964), 43.
2. John C. Carr, "An Interview with Walker Percy 1971," in *Conversations with Walker Percy* (Jackson, MS: University Press of Mississippi, 1985), 60.
3. *Boswell's Life of Johnson* (London: Oxford University Press, 1931), I, 366.
4. Simon, *A General Theory of Authority* (Notre Dame, IN: University of Notre Dame Press, 1980), 112.
5. Ibid., 137.

Appendix III
1. Giovanni Boccaccio, "Dante," in *The World's Great Catholic Literature,* ed. George Schuster (Harrison, CO: Roman Catholic Books, 1942), 106–7.
2. Lewis, *An Experiment in Criticism* (Cambridge: Cambridge University Press, [1961] 2002), 140–41.
3. Anthony Trollope, *Barchester Towers* (New York: Signet, [1857] 1963), 59.
4. Wodehouse, *The World of Wodehouse Clergy* (London: Hutchinson, 1984), 237.
5. Chesterton, "Why I Am a Catholic," in *G. K. Chesterton: Collected Works* (San Francisco: Ignatius Press, 1990), Vol. III, 129.
6. *Josef Pieper—An Anthology* (San Francisco: Ignatius Press, 1989).
7. Dennis Quinn, Iris Exiled: A Synoptic History of Wonder (Lanham, MD: University Press of America, 2002), 118.

Bibliography

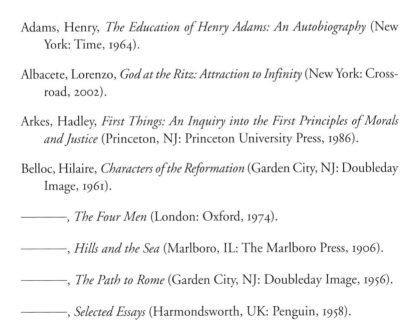

Adams, Henry, *The Education of Henry Adams: An Autobiography* (New York: Time, 1964).

Albacete, Lorenzo, *God at the Ritz: Attraction to Infinity* (New York: Crossroad, 2002).

Arkes, Hadley, *First Things: An Inquiry into the First Principles of Morals and Justice* (Princeton, NJ: Princeton University Press, 1986).

Belloc, Hilaire, *Characters of the Reformation* (Garden City, NJ: Doubleday Image, 1961).

———, *The Four Men* (London: Oxford, 1974).

———, *Hills and the Sea* (Marlboro, IL: The Marlboro Press, 1906).

———, *The Path to Rome* (Garden City, NJ: Doubleday Image, 1956).

———, *Selected Essays* (Harmondsworth, UK: Penguin, 1958).

———, *Selected Essays of Hilaire Belloc* (London: Methuen, 1941).

Berry, Wendell, *A Place on Earth: Revision* (New York: Farrar, 1983).

Birzer, Bradley J., *J. R. R. Tolkien's Sanctifying Myth: Understanding Middle-earth* (Wilmington, DE: ISI Books, 2003).

Bloom, Allan, *The Closing of the American Mind* (New York: Simon & Schuster, 1987).

———, with Harry Jaffa, *Shakespeare's Politics* (Chicago: University of Chicago Press, 1981).

Bochenski, J. M., *Philosophy: An Introduction* (New York: Harper, 1972).

Boswell's Life of Johnson (London: Oxford, 1931).

Budziszewski, J., *Written on the Heart: The Case for Natural Law* (Downer's Grove, IL: Inter-Varsity Press, 1997).

Burleigh, Anne, *Journey Up the River* (San Francisco: Ignatius Press, 1994).

Cather, Willa, *Death Comes for the Archbishop* (New York: Vintage, 1973).

Chesterton, G. K., *Collected Works* (San Francisco: Ignatius Press, 1986–Present).

———, "On the Classics," in *Come to Think of It* (New York: Dodd, Mead, 1931), 53–58.

Cicero, *On the Good Life*, ed. Michael Grant (Harmondsworth, UK: Penguin, 1979).

———, *Selected Works*, ed. Michael Grant (Harmondsworth, UK: Penguin, 1960).

Clemens, Samuel L., *Life on the Mississippi* (New York: Lancer, 1968).

Craven, Margaret, *Again Calls the Owl* (New York: Laurel, 1980).

Deane, Herbert, *The Political and Social Ideas of St. Augustine* (New York: Columbia University Press, 1956).

Dudley, Owen Francis, *The Shadow on the Earth* (London: Longmans, 1926).

Emberley, Peter, and Barry Cooper, eds., *Faith and Political Philosophy: The Correspondence Between Leo Strauss and Eric Voegelin*, (University Park, PA: Pennsylvania State University Press, 1993).

Fortin, Ernest L., *Collected Works*, ed. J. Brian Benestad (Lanham, MD: Rowman & Littlefield, 1996), 3 vols.

Fowler, H. W., *Dictionary of Modern English Usage*, ed. Sir Ernest Gowers (New York: Oxford, 1965).

Gilson, Étienne, *God and Philosophy* (New Haven, CT: Yale University Press, 1941).

——, *Reason and Revelation in the Middle Ages* (New York: Scribner's, 1938).

——, *The Unity of Philosophical Experience* (San Francisco: Ignatius Press, [1937] 1999).

Guardini, Romano, *The End of the Modern World* (Wilmington, DE: ISI Books, 1998).

Heidegger, Martin, *What Is Philosophy?* Trans., J. Wilde and W. Klubak (New Haven, CT: Yale University Press, 1956).

Highet, Gilbert, *Poets in a Landscape: Great Latin Poets in the Italy of Today* (London: Hamish Hamilton, 1957).

Hittinger, John P., *Liberty, Wisdom, and Grace* (Lanham, MD: Lexington Books, 2002).

Hittinger, Russell, *The First Grace: Rediscovering the Natural Law in a Post-Christian World* (Wilmington, DE: ISI Books, 2002).

Houselander, Caryle, *Guilt* (New York: Sheed & Ward, 1951).

Jaki, Stanley L., *Chance or Reality and Other Essays* (Wilmington, DE: ISI Books, 1986).

―――, *The Limits of a Limitless Science* (Wilmington, DE: ISI Books, 2000).

Johnson, Paul, *The Intellectuals* (New York: Knopf, 1988).

Johnson, Samuel, *Selected Essays* (London: Penguin, 2003).

Kass, Leon R., *The Hungry Soul: Eating and the Perfection of Our Nature* (New York: The Free Press, 1994).

Kraynak, Robert P., *Christian Faith and Modern Democracy: God and Politics in the Fallen World* (Notre Dame, IN: University of Notre Dame Press, 2001).

Kreeft, Peter, *C. S. Lewis for the Third Millennium* (San Francisco: Ignatius Press, 1994).

―――, *The Philosophy of Tolkien* (San Francisco: Ignatius Press, 2004).

L'Amour, Louis, *The Education of a Wandering Man* (New York: Bantam, 1990).

Langan, Thomas, *The Catholic Tradition* (Columbia, MD: University of Missouri Press, 1998).

Lawler, Peter Augustine, *Aliens in America: The Strange Truth About Our Souls* (Wilmington, DE: ISI Books, 2002).

Lazarus, Mel, *Miss Peach, Again* (New York: Grosset, 1972).

Lewis, C. S., *An Experiment in Criticism* (London: Cambridge, 2002).

―――, *Christian Reflections* (Grand Rapids, MI: Eerdmans, 1982).

―――, *God in the Dock: Essays on Theology and Ethics* (Grand Rapids, MI: Eerdmans, 1989).

————, *Mere Christianity* (New York: Macmillan, 1975).

————, *Till We Have Faces* (Grand Rapids, MI: Eerdmans, 1970).

————, *The Weight of Glory* (New York: Macmillan, 1980).

Lunn, Arnold, *Now I See* (New York: Sheed & Ward, 1938).

Mahoney, Daniel J., *DeGaulle: Statesmanship, Grandeur, and Modern Democracy* (Westport, CT: Praeger, 1996).

Maritain, Jacques, *The Education of Man: The Educational Philosophy of Jacques Maritain*, eds. Donald and Idella Gallagher (Garden City, NJ: Doubleday, 1962).

McGinley, Phyllis, "On the Consolations of Illiteracy," *Saturday Review Reader,* Number 3 (New York: Bantam, 1950).

McInerny, Ralph, *The Very Rich Hours of Jacques Maritain: A Spiritual Life* (Notre Dame, IN: University of Notre Dame Press, 2003).

McNabb, Vincent, *The Church and Philosophy* (London: Macmillan, 1927).

Meilaender, Gilbert C., *Friendship: A Study in Theological Ethics* (Notre Dame, IN: University of Notre Dame Press, 1981).

Morse, Jennifer Roback, *Love and Economics* (Dallas: Spence, 2001).

Murphy, G. Ronald, *The Owl, the Raven, and the Dove: The Religious Meaning of the Grimms' Magic Fairy Tales* (New York: Oxford, 2000).

Myrer, Anton, *Once an Eagle* (New York: Berkeley Medallion, 1968).

Newman, John Henry, *The Idea of a University* (Garden City, NJ: Doubleday Image, 1959).

————, *Parochial and Plain Sermons* (San Francisco: Ignatius Press, [1891] 1987).

Nietzsche, Frederick, *Beyond Good and Evil* (Harmondsworth, UK: Penguin, 1976).

O'Brien, Michael, *Children of the Last Days* (San Francisco: Ignatius Press, 1996–98), 6 vols.

O'Connor, Flannery, *Letters of Flannery O'Connor: The Habit of Being*, ed., Sally Fitzgerald (New York: Vintage, 1979).

Pearce, Joseph, *Old Thunder: A Life of Hilaire Belloc* (London: Harper Collins, 2002).

Percy, Walker, *Conversations with Walker Percy*, eds. Lewis Lawson and Victor Kramer (Jackson, MS: University of Mississippi Press, 1985).

———, *The Correspondence of Shelby Foote & Walker Percy*, ed. Jay Tolson (New York: Norton, 1997).

Pieper, Josef, *In Defense of Philosophy* (San Francisco: Ignatius Press, 1992).

———, *Faith, Hope, Love* (San Francisco: Ignatius Press, 1997).

———, *Guide to Thomas Aquinas* (San Francisco: Ignatius Press, 1991).

———, *Josef Pieper—An Anthology* (San Francisco: Ignatius Press, 1989).

———, *Leisure: The Basis of Culture* (South Bend, IN: St. Augustine's Press, 1998).

———, *Living the Truth (The Truth of All Things* and *Reality and the Good)* (San Francisco: Ignatius Press, 1989).

———, *Problems of Modern Faith*, trans. J. Van Heureck (Chicago: Franciscan Herald Press, 1974).

———, *In Tune with the World: A Theory of Festivity* (Chicago: Franciscan Herald Press, 1973).

Purcell, Brendan M., *The Drama of Humanity: Towards a Philosophy of Humanity in History* (New York: Peter Lang, 1996).

Quinn, Dennis, *Iris Exiled: A Synoptic History of Wonder* (Lanham, MD: University Press of America, 2002).

Ratzinger, Josef, *Salt of the Earth: An Interview with Peter Seewald* (San Francisco: Ignatius Press, 1997).

———, *The Spirit of the Liturgy* (San Francisco: Ignatius Press, 2000).

Redpath, Peter A., *Wisdom's Odyssey* (Amsterdam: Rodopi, 1997).

Reilly, Robert R., *Surprised by Beauty: A Listener's Guide to the Recovery of Modern Music* (Washington: Morley Books, 2002).

Rousseau, Jean-Jacques, *The Reveries of the Solitary Walker*, trans. C. Butterworth (New York: Harper Colophon, 1979).

Rowland, Tracey, *Culture and the Thomist Tradition* (London: Routledge, 2003).

Sayers, Dorothy L., *The Whimsical Christian* (New York: Macmillan, 1978).

Sandoz, Ellis, *Political Apocalypse: A Study of Dostoevsky's Grand Inquisitor* (Wilmington, DE: ISI Books, 2000).

———, *The Politics of Truth and Other Untimely Essays* (Columbia, MO: University of Missouri Press, 1999).

———, *The Voegelinian Revolution* (Baton Rouge, LA: Louisiana State University Press, 1981).

Saward, John, *The Beauty of Holiness and the Holiness of Beauty* (San Francisco: Ignatius Press, 1997).

Schall, James V., *A Student's Guide to Liberal Learning* (Wilmington, DE: ISI Books, 1997).

————, *Another Sort of Learning* (San Francisco: Ignatius Press, 1989).

————, *At the Limits of Political Philosophy* (Washington: Catholic University of America Press, 1996).

————, *Idylls and Rambles: Lighter Christian Essays* (San Francisco: Ignatius Press, 1994).

————, *On the Unseriousness of Human Affairs: Teaching, Writing, Playing, Believing, Lecturing, Philosophizing, Singing, Dancing* (Wilmington, DE: ISI Books, 2001).

————, *The Praise of Sons of Bitches: On the Worship of God by Fallen Men* (Slough, UK: St Paul Publications, 1978).

————, *Schall on Chesterton: Timely Essays on Timeless Paradoxes* (Washington: Catholic University of America Press, 2000).

Schulz, Charles, *Could You Be More Pacific?* (New York: Topper Books, 1988).

————, *Here Comes Charlie Brown* (New York: Fawcett, 1957).

Schumacher, E. F., *A Guide for the Perplexed* (New York: Harper Colophon, 1977).

Schindler, David, *Heart of the World, Center of the Church* (Grand Rapids, MI: Eerdmans, 1996).

Scruton, Roger, *The West and the Rest* (Wilmington, DE: ISI Books, 2001).

Sertillanges, A. D., *The Intellectual Life* (Washington: The Catholic University of America Press, 1998).

Sheed, Frank, *Sidelights on the Catholic Revival* (New York: Sheed & Ward, 1940).

Simon, Julian L., *The Ultimate Resource 2* (Princeton, NJ: Princeton University Press, 1997).

Simon, Yves, *A General Theory of Authority* (Notre Dame, IN: University of Notre Dame Press, 1980).

Sokolowski, Robert, *Eucharistic Presence: A Study of the Theology of Disclosure* (Washington: Catholic University of America Press, 1994).

———, *The God of Faith and Reason* (Washington: Catholic University of America Press, 1996).

Strauss, Leo, *City and Man* (Chicago: University of Chicago Press, 1964).

———, *Liberalism: Ancient and Modern* (Chicago: University of Chicago Press, 1968).

———, *Studies in Platonic Political Philosophy*, ed. Thomas Pangle (Chicago: University of Chicago Press, 1983).

———, *Thoughts on Machiavelli* (Glencoe, IL: The Free Press, 1958).

Thurber, James, *My Life and Hard Times* (New York: Bantam, 1968).

Tolkien, J. R. R., *The Letters of J. R. R. Tolkien*, ed. Humphrey Carpenter (New York: Houghton Mifflin, 1981).

———, *The Lord of the Rings* (New York: Ballantine, 1994), 3 vols.

———, *The Tolkien Reader* (New York: Ballantine, 1966).

Trollope, Anthony, *Barchester Towers* (New York: Signet, [1857] 1963).

Voegelin, Eric, *Conversations with Eric Voegelin*, ed. R. Eric O'Connor (Montreal: Thomas More Papers 76, 1980).

———, *Plato* (Columbia, MO: University of Missouri Press, 2001).

Wallace, William A., *The Modeling of Nature: Philosophy of Science and Philosophy of Nature in Synthesis* (Washington: Catholic University of America Press, 1996).

Walsh, David, *The Third Millennium: Reflections on Faith and Reason* (Washington: Georgetown University Press, 1989).

Waugh, Evelyn, *A Little Learning: An Autobiography* (Boston: Little, Brown, 1964).

————, *Brideshead Revisited* (Boston, Little, Brown, 1945).

Weigel, George, *Witness to Hope: The Biography of Pope John Paul II* (New York: HarperCollins, 1999).

Wilhelmsen, Frederick D., "Great Books: Enemies of Wisdom?" *Modern Age* 31 (Summer/Fall 1987), 323–31.

————, *The Paradoxical Structure of Existence* (Albany, NY: Preserving Christian Publications, 1995).

Wodehouse, P. G., *How Right You Are, Jeeves* (New York: Avon, 1976).

————, *Pearls, Girls, and Monte Bodkin* (London: Pennyfarthing Edition, 1972).

————, *The World of Wodehouse Clergy* (London: Hutchinson, 1984).

Wojtyla, Karol (John Paul II), *Crossing the Threshold of Hope* (New York: Knopf, 1994).

World's Great Catholic Literature, ed. George Schuster (Harrison, CO: Roman Catholic Books, 1942).

Index

Index

Index

Index

Index

walking and, 93
what is and, xvi
wisdom and, 48, 52
Sokolowski, Robert, 88, 159
solitude, walking and, 96
Sophists, 5, 163
soul, 34
    flatness of, 115, 120
    knowledge and, 10
    order in, 5, 34–35, 62–63, 164–65
    spiritual power of, 10
specialization, 145–46
"Speech on Conciliation" (Burke), 68
Spitzer, Robert, 162
sports, 57–58, 172–73
Stalin, Josef, 15, 16–17, 20
Stoicism, 80, 83
Strangers and Sojourners (O'Brien), 15–16
Strauss, Leo, 26, 83, 128, 164, 165, 168, 174
Strunk, William, 5, 7
St. Thomas Aquinas (Chesterton), 17, 159, 169
Student's Guide to Liberal Learning, A (Schall), xv, 17
suffering, value of, 140
Summa Theologiae (Aquinas), 10, 83
Surprised by Beauty (Reilly), 160
Symposium (Plato), xvi, 52, 148

teaching
    art of, 162
    end of, 163
    error and, 162
    public life and, 166–67
    quality in, 165–66
    truth and, 163
    writing and, 162

technology, 3, 175
television, 114–15, 120, 175
Teresa of Avila, St., 174
That Hideous Strength (Lewis), 16
theology, philosophy and, 174
thinking
    Aquinas, St. Thomas, and, 144
    joys and travails of, xi, 1–6
    life of the mind and, xii
    order in, 74
    pleasure and, 82
    reading and, xiii
Thrasymachus, 147
Thucydides, 52
Thurber, James, 131
Tibullus, 49
tolerance
    philosophy and, 150
    truth and, 123, 129
Tolkien, Christopher, 112
Tolkien, J. R. R., 54–55, 88, 112–13, 168
"Trade Winds" (Cerf), 66
Treasure Island (Stevenson), 8
Trollope, Anthony, 71, 180, 181
"Trumans Leave the White House, The" (Brown), 66
truth
    affirmation of, 124, 145
    as dangerous, 149
    desire for, 9–10
    error and, 65
    existence of, 122–25, 125–28
    freedom and, 36
    life of the mind and, xii, 144
    possibility of, 120
    purpose of, 127
    reading and, 1
    as relative, 123, 125
    teaching and, 163

About the Author

James V. Schall, S.J., is Professor of Government at Georgetown University. He is the author of numerous books, including *Another Sort of Learning, A Student's Guide to Liberal Learning,* and *On the Unseriousness of Human Affairs.*